C000008084

<u>Acknowledgements</u>

To Louise Young for many arduous hours
To Jayne Brewster-Beard for the magnificent illustrations.
To Bill May for the cover drawing.
To David Fowkes & Julie Moore for their painstaking help and guidance
throughout.

<u>Dedicated</u>

To my dear wife Margaret for her patience throughout and our daughter
Ellen with love.

Published by

Richard Papworth
2 Cloverslade
Findern Heights
Findern
Derbyshire
DE65 6QF

ISBN 0-9538672-0-X

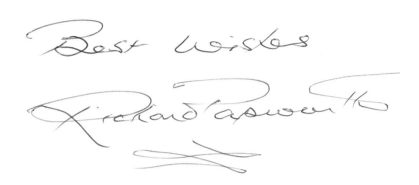

'KEY MAN'

BY

RICHARD PAPWORTH

LIST OF CONTENTS

PREFACE

My autobiography is intended to take readers on a guided tour of my working life.

I do not profess to have achieved anything remarkable or outstanding, in fact quite the opposite – looked at in those terms I may be seen as an under achiever. However, one thing I do profess is to have done something different than many, and that is to have been involved in the upkeep of law and order in its various guises throughout my adult life.

I began as a Police Cadet until having to join the army serving as a Military Policeman until demob, afterwards experiencing county and city life as a Policeman.

Finding county policing offered me a wide variety of work but not so with city policing. So after 'shaking hands' with thousands of door knobs by night and being required to stick vile tasting brown paper onto car tyres by day – and very little else, I decided that city life as a policeman was not for me. I resigned to become a detective in a large multiple store – an interesting job and full of action which I explain in the book, but offering no future prospects so I applied for and was accepted by H. M. Prison Service, to which I devote most of the book.

Serving for thirty years at both high and low security category establishments dealing with both adult and young offenders I have had many experiences, dealt with plenty of incidents and suffered the ups and downs whilst striving to reach middle management.

There are plenty of humorous events, which are highlighted by a series of excellent cartoons drawn by a well-known local artist.

Much of my book relates to working in Birmingham and Derbyshire prisons also Onley young offenders' institution.

Events are recalled of working in the aftermath of a riot and setting up a fully operational prison in six days from a disused Vietnamese boat camp.

My hope is not only to give my readers an insight into how a prison works, but also to make it entertaining and amusing.

If you find that sometimes I revert to prison jargon I have included a simple glossary at the front of the book to explain their meanings.

Although dealing with unwilling guests calls for tact and integrity, I find it is essential to maintain a balanced sense of humour to enable staff to cope with the inevitable pressures a job like this creates.

PRISON SLANG

Useful abbreviations of terminology used within this book:

APPS	Governors Applications
BANG UP	Locked Up
BARON	Drugs Tobacco Supplier
BEAST	Sex Offender
BENDER	Suspended Sentence
BIRD	Imprisonment
BLOCK	Segregation Unit
BOSS	Officer of the Prison
BURN	Tobacco
C.C.	Capital Charge or Cellular Confinement
CANTEEN	Prison Shop
CHIV	Weapon
CHOKEY	Restrictive Diet No.1 – Bread and Water
CON	Convicted Prisoner or Pulling a Fast One
DADDY	As Baron, But in Borstal
DEAR JOHN	Bad Letter
GATED	Gate Arrest
GENT	Confidence Trickster
GHOSTED	Transfer to Another Prison without Notice
GRASS	Informer or Cannabis
H	Heroin
HARD NUT	Strong Arm Men for Barons
HEAVY MOB	Staff Attending Alarm Call
HOOCH	Illicit Alcohol
JAM ROLL	Parole
JELLY	Gelignite
JUDAS WINDOW	Cell Observation Glass
KB	Refusal of Parole
LABOUR	Work in Prison
LEGGED	Escaped
NICK	Prison
NICKED	Placed on a Disciplinary Report
NONCE	Sex Offender

NO 1	Governing Governor
OVER THE WALL	Escaped
PAD	Cell
PETER	Cell
PLANT	Some Item (Illegal) Hidden by Another Prisoner in Someone Else's Cell or Kit
PORRIDGE	Imprisonment
RECESS	Ablutions
RUB DOWN	Quick Search
SCARPER	Abscond
SCREW	Prisoner Officer
SHIP OUT	Quick Transfer as Ghosted
SHIT	Cannabis
SKIDS	Underwear
SPIN	Search
SKY PILOT	Vicar
SLOP OUT	Morning Ritual of Emptying Chamber Pots and Drawing Water
SNOUT	Tobacco
STITCH UP	Being Made to Look Guilty of Someone Else's Offence
TOPPED	Executed or Suicide
TURNOVER	Full Scale Search
VALS	Valuable Property

CONSTABULARIES AND BEFORE

Growing Up

1935 was a very uneventful year, except for the fact that I was born. I don't remember too much about it though. However one thing I do remember is my lucky escape. Having been born on the fourteenth of February, I was nearly named "Valentine," phew!

As the years passed, I became involved in the usual mischief lads get involved in. I vividly recall falling into a brook regularly, and dependent on the type of vegetables being canned at the time, would determine the colour of which my friends and I sported to our homes. Mothers could always tell what was being prepared, I think beetroot and carrots were the most colourful. The reason we used to fall in was because of the dares to jump from the rails, to the crumbling bank on the opposite side, which often led to disaster.

I played both football and cricket and was fairly good, so I became a member of both teams, which used to let us off lessons when matches were on.

A large part of my schooling was during the war years and many restrictions were imposed. As lads we didn't take too much notice, I can however, recall us having periodically to wear a Mickey Mouse gas mask, and enter a big van which emitted gas to ensure the mask was gas proof. Not a happy experience, which usually made our eyes sting.

The only criminal activity I got up to, was scrumping a few apples. But always getting caught, I decided I would not make a good criminal, and therefore, I would go to the other side of the fence.

On leaving school I became a van boy delivering laundry. I now understand why my driver used to take so long delivering the packages to attractive young ladies, I wonder if this is what was meant when they talked about washing dirty linen in public?

Anyhow, after a spell cleaning and firing railway engines I left and this is where my story really begins.

Cadet

I'm still puzzled at my acceptance, but I managed it, I was taken on as a police cadet with the then, 'Hunts County Police.' This was a relatively new venture and most of the other cadets were better educationally qualified than I. Perhaps they were looking for someone different and I certainly fitted the bill.

In real terms the cadet was the dogs body and battering ram from anyone above them, which was virtually everyone.

My first posting was to Huntingdon, a small but busy market town with a constant flow of traffic, particularly heavy goods vehicles, passing through the narrow high street frequently causing bottlenecks, particularly on race days.

Most of the cadet's work was inside the police station office, dealing with an antiquated switchboard, which, if leads were shorted, gave you a nasty jolt. I would like as many pounds, as times, I have pulled out the wrong wires and cut off two conversations. This, much to my superiors' wrath, if given their wish would long since have despatched me to my maker.

The enquiry office was my introduction into learning how to handle people from all walks of life, from the angry person, to the helpless. Some would demand action yesterday and blame you for their misfortunes. The secret was to listen and not bite back!

The most common things dealt with were lost and found property, accident production of insurance and driving documents, and listening to complainants and passing them over to the appropriate people.

Very occasionally we would be allowed to accompany a police officer on his beat, or a tour in a patrol car and sometimes help out with servicing the always-shiny patrol cars. I found out why, we often had to clean them!

In the early stages I dreaded the thought of seeing, let alone handling a dead person, and if a sudden death were being processed, I would always steer well clear. One day the inevitable happened. "Richard, I want you to be here this afternoon, and take the undertakers to the mortuary to collect the body of that bloke who died in the buffer depot. They are coming from Preston." My mind raced ahead, scheming up a way of avoiding this job. I know, I'll take some Civil Defence letters for delivery and when I arrive back the coast will be clear. My excuse being that I was delayed in contacting people and all would be well. It was a beautiful afternoon so I took my time.

When I arrived back at the police station much later, I was met by a very angry Sergeant, "Where the bloody hell have you been?" "Delivering letters Sarge," I replied. "Have they gone?" At this stage the enquiry office door opened,* "I've come for the body," the Sarge was almost pleasant; "Off you go Richard."

Well, my plans had been foiled, but still racing ahead, my mind was working overtime. I've unlocked dads padlock on the shed before, so I'll just unlock this place and move to one side so that the undertakers can do their job, then I still won't have to see the body.

I mounted my cycle and led the hearse to our mortuary; it was just alongside the cemetery. I entered the gate and unlocked the padlock and readied myself to move aside as planned, but the two undertakers grasped my arms, quickly led me to the body, whipped off the sheet and placed my hands upon it. From that day to this I have handled many dead people and have completely lost my fear of dealing with death. So I have much reason to be grateful to those two undertakers, who I imagine have since become customers of others in their trade.

Superiors seemed to take great delight in deflating the ego of us young lads. I clearly remember an armistice parade, I was smart and feeling very important, but my mates were grouped together taking the mickey. Both they and I knew that a cadet had no power, had I had power then I'm sure I would have run them in that day.

Up comes the Chief's car and as I opened the door, smartly saluted him, so he emerged handing me a clothes brush because his back was covered in dog hairs. This tickled my mates whom started laughing uncontrollably. They were moved on by a real copper only to relate the entire incident over a pint at some later time to a full house.

This was embarrassing, but the second incident took some beating. I was ordered to go to the town's ironmonger to collect an item for my Chief Inspector. In those days you questioned nothing, so, as ordered I

---

* See illustration one "I've come for the body"

11

presented myself there and requested the package. This was handed to me in the shape of an unwrapped china chamber pot. This was too much, "Can't you wrap it" I enquired, "Sorry," he said. So off I go keeping in to the side of the street. I was just congratulating myself on meeting no one I knew and confidently strode into the road leading to the police station, when up pulls a lorry and the laughter started – My father and uncle! It took a lot of living down for months afterwards, comments such as, *"Oh, you've got a handle to your name" or, "I didn't know that part of your kit was a jerry." Like everything it faded, but the memory still remains.

By now nothing could shock me and I was largely cured from blushing except in the company of the opposite sex.

I learned much as a police cadet and saw many different officers at work; each had a different style. Some adopted a hard line approach, others an easy going approach, those, who by their very size made villains cringe and those in contrast who were less physically blessed, used their ability to talk to people rather than become physical or threatening. A police force needed this variety.

One technique I learned, was the, I know you approach, used when you needed information from someone whose identity you were unsure of. You would say something like, "I know who you are, your Bill Brown from Coronation Street." Inadvertently the person would respond saying, "No I'm Charlie Smith from High Street," giving you the desired information without realising it. Obviously this technique only worked once, because once bitten twice shy.

Unfortunately, throughout life I have been a somewhat stormy character, but an object lesson I quickly learnt was that as a policeman, or in any like type of occupation, once you lose your self-control you have lost the battle, because you are not able to rationalise or to think clearly. Prisoners as I was to discover later in life were experts at winding up, especially if they thought you would bite.

I think that as the years have passed I have mellowed, although sometimes I think that my wife would dispute this!

I was to find out that most police officers were very human with a difficult job to perform. Although some had ulterior motives, for example, an Inspector in command of one station I worked regularly would instruct me to bring forty churchmen and an ounce of pipe tobacco

---

* See illustration two "Oh, you've got a handle on your name"

each Friday from the local tobacconist in my hometown. He would give these to an old road sweeper. I thought that this was generosity in the extreme, until I discovered that the old man was an excellent informant because he saw everything. What the Inspector didn't know, was that the old man also tipped the criminal fraternity if the police were around. A double agent if you like!

As a cadet you had no actual powers, but you were there to observe. You were also a scapegoat, or if you like, the butt of every practical joke. One older officer took to growing, cultivating and smoking his own brand of home-grown tobacco. Most of the officers kept well away from him in the station because the smell was awful, except of course for the cadet who was rooted to the switchboard. He had to suffer in silence, whilst the officer took great delight in blowing great clouds of this foul smelling mixture, so it slowly drifted up and around you, amidst great bursts of deep throated laughter.

The main idea of the cadet scheme was to give an insight into the work of a police officer, with a view to encouraging the right type of person to join the police in the future.

Unfortunately, National Service interrupted the process, because at this time it was compulsory for all young men to undergo two years training even police cadets who, as I completed my service were exempted.

National Service

My introduction to this was something I will not forget, saying goodbye to my home ties and travelling by train to Northampton, because I was going to be an infantryman in the Northants Regiment.

After handing my ticket in, I made my way to a group of lads standing alongside an army lorry. A very smart orderly Sergeant, who approached us in an amicable manner, asked us to identify ourselves and get into the back of the lorry. We were driven to the depot of the Northants Regiment. This is where the pleasantries ceased and the screaming started "Get fell in, stand still, keep quiet. New intake, new intake shun." An officer approaches, slightly older but certainly not on our side, "Welcome gentlemen to the home of the Northants." He then entered into a dialogue of do's and don'ts, finishing off he handed us over to a Sergeant Major, whom before we knew it, had us marched over to the stores and changed into khaki. He doubled us over to a bleak looking barrack room saying, "This is your new home, it's not a stately one, but it bloody well won't be far short by the time you have finished cleaning it." At this stage of the game I was thinking about going AWOL (absent without leave), but common sense prevailed and I stayed the course. One jumped up little corporal had it in for me, but very soon I was to be transferred to the Royal Military Police and I swore that one-day I would exact my revenge.

I was glad to get away, but found that if I thought that the Northants was strict, I was in for an even bigger shock. However, having been faced with eighteen weeks of hard training, including two haircuts in one day, thus* looking somewhat like a billiard ball, I still managed to survive.

During this time we were trained in handling motorcycles and lorries, shooting rifle, pistol, Bren and Sten guns, negotiating difficult assault courses, traffic control and above all drill, drill and more drill.

Of the guns, the Bren gun was like a Rolls Royce to handle, but the Sten gun was an absolute death trap if it wasn't held correctly. As for the pistol, well after seeing all the films of marksmen hitting their targets continually, I should have been at the very back of the queue as I found them extremely difficult to use.

On the motorcycles we were introduced to confidence riding. Nobody's going to make me do that I thought, but they did. I think mainly from fear. We had to stand on the saddle, lay on the petrol tank and crouch on the footrest. All done to a whistle of command rather like something from a ballet with about thirty of us doing the same sort of stunts.

Also a criss-cross of motorcycles one coming from one corner of the field and the other the opposite corner, the objective being to pass at the centre but very close to each other. When this was demonstrated by the instructors they collided, luckily no one was hurt and only minimal damage done. Certain threats were offered to anyone daring to reveal these secret mishaps, so our lips remained sealed. They actually brought the cakes for a week. This was something unheard of before.

Eventually the training was completed and at our passing out parade, would have given a guards regiment, a good run for their money in terms of precision. Throughout the course we had been guided and fathered by our squad instructor and we dared not put a foot wrong. You could see the

---

* See illustration three "Looking somewhat like a billiard ball"

pride etched on his face and no one let him down. We didn't dare!

He joined us in a celebration at the local pub afterwards. We couldn't afford much, other than a pint and a sandwich. On army wages of twenty-one shillings a week, anything more elaborate would have been too expensive.

Off on a short home leave after which many returned to receive postings to Cyprus, Korea, Kenya and Malaysia. All of us had received the relevant injections to enable us to be sent anywhere in the World. However an overseas posting wasn't for me, as I was posted to Colchester, a garrison town, housing a wide variety of regiments. Most of which were either waiting or returning from postings. Colchester also played host to the notorious military prison.

Our main duty was to keep military law. Most personnel were well behaved, as military law was so strict, that only a few wished to grace the inside of the glasshouse, this is how a military prison was known. Regimes inside these establishments were very strict indeed.

There are however exceptions to every rule and one time that trouble could be expected, was when a company returned from overseas service and their pay had been delayed. You could then expect in-discipline in many ways. I have seen soldier's hi-jack vehicles, block streets and use many other ways to attract attention to their plight.

One of the better jobs was a coastal patrol of East Anglia. The redcap uniform seemed to attract the girls who saw many eligible bachelors amongst its ranks.

I faced many potentially violent situations and quickly learned when discretion became the better part of valour.

Towards the end of my service I returned to the training depot and trained as a regimental signaller. This was a very interesting course, learning how to set up communications, mainly in the field, Morse code and the operation of 19 and 22 radio sets. We had numerous field exercises, which besides being fun, much was learnt.

Time flew by and before I knew it I was due for demob.

Much of our time was taken up in dealing with the Army Emergency Reserve lads, who like us had completed their time and had to become members of the A.E.R. This included a two-week camp each summer, which many converted to two weeks holiday.

They couldn't really care less about military discipline, because in two weeks time they would once again be civilians.

Most of them were well behaved but if any trouble did arise, then usually it would happen during the last few days. Our role was one of containment and pacification.

Whilst on mobile patrol, I was once travelling as a passenger when the vehicle we were patrolling, went out of control, hit a ditch and landing upside down in a police officers front garden. From what I can gather, the officer was more concerned about his flowers than the occupants of the army Champ. The driver eventually went on to become a test driver for a top car manufacturer and a T.T. rider, where I'm told he sadly met his end.

I did ride passenger to him once on an improvised track and despite the rough ground managed to survive. I wouldn't have missed the experience, but was glad to get off in one piece.

Duty in detachments was pretty easy going, then one day the Battalion Regimental Sergeant Major decided that all staff would parade in running kit. This to undergo a cross-country run, no excuses were acceptable and the shapes and sizes that appeared, were unbelievable and certainly in need of trimming.

There were cooks, clerks, and drill sergeants, store men, medics and police no one was spared. "I'll sort the men from the boys," and he certainly did, I was one of the boys.

Whilst serving in the forces, I could never had imagined, that a leave spent at a colleagues home, was destined to completely change my life.

One evening we were becoming bored, so he suggested that he take me out to meet one of his friends! Thinking that this was one of his mates I agreed. Not in my wildest dreams did I imagine that his friend would be a very pretty dark haired young lady, with eyes that literally talked. No wonder one of her favourite records was 'Spanish Eyes.' Had I have been aware, I think that I may have opted out because basically I was a shy person.

Margaret the young lady I refer to, was busy watching a television play, but not for long, following our intrusion.

I think for me, it was love at first sight, however I don't think it was for Margaret. I just grew on her. I couldn't sleep,' desperately hoping we would meet again. We did and our courtship followed, much of which was by letter, as seeing each other was much rarer than that of most couples.

When we did meet, it was a real treat, to see her style of dress, made me feel and look precisely what I was, a real country bumpkin.

Anyway, we eventually got married and after fifty plus years we are still together, which is much more than many can say. I think that the part of our vows, 'Till death do us part' will apply I'm sure unconditionally.

Life has generally been good to us, but has not always run a smooth path. We have had our fair share of 'ups and downs,' but one thing I am absolutely certain of is that I couldn't have had a better partner to share it with. It is for this very reason that I dedicate my book to her, with very grateful thanks.

The Counties

After serving in the army and taking my fair share of discipline, you would have thought that I would just want to settle down into a quiet type of office job. But no, not me, being a glutton for punishment I applied for a second dose, by joining my home County Police force. More drill, more PE, more yelling and bawling by instructors wishing to imprint a further mark of authority upon me. But to be quite honest, I found this tame by comparison to the army and being fit and keen I was raring to go.

The course was intense and each lunchtime you were given an hour to walk around the grounds of this beautiful hall, which had been converted in a police training school, to learn parrot fashion, every single power of arrest and definition of offences. To look at us you would have thought that we were rehearsing a play. The system must have worked because even to this day, I remember quite a number of them. However, as at the beginning you were in the junior squad progressing through to the intermediate and then final stages. During this you were trained in all aspects of police work both theory and practical.

The then Home Secretary who addressed us later took our final passing out parade. This was a very important day not only for us, as it marked the start of our new career, but also for him, as it was the very day he had to decide whether or not a woman should go to the gallows for the murder of her aristocratic lover.

She was duly executed. The last woman in Britain. If I were to offer an opinion it would be that far worse criminals have escaped the ultimate penalty committing far worse murders.

As with all courses they end when examinations and this was no exception. An exam was taken at the three stages. For some reason, maybe not paying attention or nerves, I came out very low on the first and easiest exam. So I really put an effort into the intermediate and final ones, coming out in the top four in one and top in the other. Whilst at home I had only just settled in when a patrol car pulled up. The officer had been instructed to take me to the Chief Constables office. Thinking I was in for a pat on the back, I complied, only to get an almighty rollicking for not trying hard enough in the first exam. I reeled back, they say that surprise is the best element of attack and I was certainly subject to this. I should have known when he kicked his dogs out of the french window of his office. A huge man with a handlebar moustache, an ex-Colonel in the Indian army, he most definitely knew how to dish out a rocket.

Life in a county force is wide and varied. A beat Constable deals with a multitude of incidents, from the minor to the very serious. One day you could be taking details of a piece of lost property, and the next be helping at a murder scene or a very serious accident.

It was the variety that I enjoyed and was to eventually spoil me for City work.

Seemingly small jobs can sometimes lead to a much more serious issue. An example would be that as a routine, quarterly we were required to submit to the motor tax authorities a list of expired road fund licences, which were identified by colour. The tax authorities would monitor if the discs had been renewed, it they hadn't a prosecution would follow and the police officer called as a witness.

Once I stopped this motorist because his disc colour did not match either the expired or new issue discs. He explained that the disc was Irish and valid in this Country. It was Irish but was not valid in this or any other Country; it was a Guinness label carefully cut out to fit into a road tax holder. On his own admission he had been using it for a considerable time. He was duly prosecuted and convicted for fraud. A policeman's son!

I am switching from one event to another to illustrate the variety of the job.

One day it was a drowning. An elderly lady who, for reasons best known to herself, had removed most of her top clothes, folded them very neatly in a churchyard whose border met the river and then have calmly walked into the river until it covered her. I imagined how that by walking into the cold water, I would have jumped out twice as quickly on impact but not this lady, she must have been very determined to end her life.

The river claimed many victims, mostly suicides but some accidents and two I call to mind. The first, when a man fooling around on some swinging boats at the local fair, lost his footing and was thrown into the river. Being a non-swimmer he drowned but an even sadder one happened, when an old school associate of mine was walking along the riverbank with his girlfriend. He heard a cry of help, diving in immediately he hit the bottom breaking his neck, so instead of marrying his sweetheart he died. The ironic twist is that the man in the water was fooling around and not in trouble at all.

Seems a morbid type of job doesn't it but much of beat police work entails, dealing with accidents and most as sad as that. I think the more you deal with the more hardened you get. The job obviously has a much lighter side to it and these are too numerous to mention.

An example would be, imagine that you are a motorist and what you see, you would not believe to be true. The police officer dismounts from his cycle, parks it, *walks up to the dustcart, brings himself up to attention and smartly salutes the man emptying someone's bin into the vehicle. Quite rightly, you would be forgiven for supposing the officer had gone mad, but he is perfectly correct in his actions. You see each week a batch of summonses are issued by the local court, which must be signed by a J.P. The chairman of the bench used to be the foreman of the dustcart and like any J.P. or magistrate was entitled to be saluted. I didn't like this because if your mates in the local, or members of the local football or cricket teams saw you, both of whom I used to play for, then you had some explaining to do.

Many of the locals lived and worked on the boats, either in the yards or transporting goods and some of course fell foul of the law. One I recall was a particularly nasty character and was extremely well known to us. An officer was sent to serve a summons upon him but lost his sea legs, after being despatched into the water by the occupant, summons and all.

---

* See illustration four "Walks up to the dustcard and smartly salutes"

I think it was more a loss of balance than an assault, as the occupant wobbled the gangplank, but we gave him the benefit of the doubt and ran him in for assault. I feel that the shock of seeing his wife wearing a fur wrap and little else could have helped.

A strange thing about this man, and I was to experience many more in later in life. Was although violent to police, usually perfectly well behaved towards prison staff, however, if he was violent towards prison staff he was less likely to be violent towards the police. This man was no exception he was a model prisoner.

Violence seemed to be less prominent in those days, probably fist fights and sometimes dirty fighting with feet and head, but weapons were an absolute rarity.

Being cheeky to your elders especially police officers, was unheard of, unfortunately, the word litigation crops up far too frequently and the timely clip of the ear has vanished. I am also speaking from experience, especially at the hands of my dear old teacher 'Fudge'.

I think that a return to showing respect to your elders would be timely along with the return of National Service, which I will talk about later. Respect costs nothing.

Much of the labour around the area was imported, mostly from Italy. There were many brickyards situated within the district along with a hostel ran by an Italian, what he didn't know about the activities within its confines was simply not worth knowing.

It was our responsibility to ensure that all the conditions of employment; residence and status were adhered to. They were obliged to notify us if they changed their address, got married and particularly if they swapped jobs. They were only officially allowed into the Country to work at the brickyards.

We were very grateful to the man who ran the hostel, as not only did he keep us well informed of hostel activities, but also of further afield and as a result a lot of crime was solved.

Alterations to their passports were not beyond the capabilities of a good forger, especially a forged stamp of authorisation.

The area was rough, but there were many good-hearted people about and when the time came for me to leave I had mixed emotions. However, move I did to Welwyn Garden City, a much busier area than I had been used to housing an arterial road within its boundaries, the A1, thus many more road traffic accidents.

The City, a model one was built in the mid- nineteen hundreds. It was the second such model City in Hertfordshire and any apparent downfalls found in the first one of Letchworth were rectified in the second. The first course of action was to build two large pubs, The Cherry Tree and The Woodman. Maybe sometimes, no pubs would have been the better option, as they produced their fair share of problems.

The City was divided into two sections by a white bridge. One side being mainly industrial and the other residential. The residential side housed many very well known people, in the fields of entertainment, politics and some related to royalty. It was only an area for the very affluent. As one can imagine these people took many holidays and presented a tempting target for the criminally minded. It was for this reason that each night, much of our time was taken up checking unoccupied premises. We had to enter all houses that were unoccupied on a pink pad and check each one meticulously, normally twice each night. We received little thanks for it, but I dread to imagine what could have transpired should something have been missed.

Also during this period, much building work was taking place and copper compounds sprung up everywhere. One officer in a section car was detailed to check at frequent intervals, he would record these in a logbook. Nothing of course usually happened so complacency crept in. The law of sod was bound to apply one day and sure enough it happened. The job was given to an older officer who signed that he had checked all compounds at say 3.00 am. Upon his return to the station, he was confronted by a very senior member of staff, who asked him when he had last carried out a check. He replied "3.00 am," but what he did not know was that two compounds had been broken into with all padlocks forced. The thieves were in custody and admitted the break-ins took place at 1.00 am, also they were arrested at 2.00 am so the officer did not have a leg to stand on. The officer's career was short lived after this. Object lesson number one: Always, be sure of your facts before committing pen to paper. Object lesson two: If the job is done properly there should not be any repercussions – there aren't any short cuts.

Saturday nights often brought its share of problems, especially in the pubs. Gangs used to travel down from London and create havoc. Our duty

Inspector got completely fed up with this and one Saturday all available manpower was mustered together. If anyone stepped slightly out of line they were searched under a local byelaw and anything resembling a weapon confiscated. These were mostly bicycle chains, some evil looking knives and even nail files, anything that could reasonably be considered as a weapon. After being fined these gangs became conspicuous by their absence and good riddance to them.

The other pub was situated on the outskirts and by comparison, was very well run, however our watch Inspector decided that one Sunday we would carry out a raid. It was rumoured that some form of gambling was taking place on the premises. I am not sure of the correct name of the game but each player threw a half a crown against one of the walls in the pub yard, the player to get his coin closest to the wall took all the other coins. This form of gambling was illegal especially in or around licensed premises. It was very funny to see grown men suddenly become Olympic athletes upon our arrival, disappearing over walls and across waste ground. One person who couldn't run was the licensee; he had to face the music along with several of his walking wounded customers, who were either physically, or due to the effects of alcohol, unable to join the mass exit of the others.

Breaking bad news was probably one of the worst jobs to befall a policeman, each time the person would open the door, probably smiling, suddenly on realising that something was wrong, would change because the officer would also be looking serious. This recognition would help to some extent as by now the person would have assumed that someone near to them had either been taken ill or died. It was certainly not a job relished by any officer.

We all had our own methods of handling this. I used to go to a neighbour and enquire as to how they got on with the person next door? If the answer was favourable, then I would most probably enlist their help to either make a cup of tea or to stay them until family arrived. I would ensure first that it was the correct person I had approached and then explain that I had some bad news. They would then wonder whom, which made the job much easier.

One Christmas day I had four of these people to deal with. It was very rare that a person became hysterical and sometimes I received a big surprise. An example of this happened when I was required to inform a lady that her husband had met his end whilst riding his motorcycle over a level crossing. She enquired if anyone was with him I advised her that a young lady had also been killed. She replied, "Serve the bastards right," and, "I'm sure you would like a cup of tea."

Apparently he was having an affair and not surprisingly she didn't approve. It certainly made my job easy.

A mysterious fatality occurred in our area and to this day I believe that it was a deliberate act. A car ploughed into a lorry parked in a lay-by, smashing its window screen and killing the driver instantly. We arrived finding the car positioned virtually at right angles embedded into the corner tailboard of the lorry.

We tested the patrol car along the same route, assuming the driver had dozed off. As the wheels hit the high kerb on three attempts, it threw the front wheels outwards and the back end toward the lay by. The only way, in which he could have succeeded in this manoeuvre, was to hold the wheel firmly and point it towards the other vehicle. Our opinion was that the incident was intended, but this was not the verdict. Accidental death was recorded. Our job was to report facts and let the authorities decide on the verdict.

A policeman's lot is not a happy one, according to a Gilbert and Sullivan opera, but it does have many lighter moments.

Animals' particularly stray dogs at that time were the responsibility of the police. On this particular day we had a very noisy dog in the kennels, his whining went on and on, their residence being outside in the station yard. The office Constable could not take it any longer and arranged for the dogs escape. Feeling very proud of himself he walked back into the office only to be confronted by a dear old lady and what did she bring? Yes the dog, "I am sure that you kind gentlemen will take care of this dog I have found wandering."

This totally deflated the office Constable and our four-legged friend recommenced his whining.

The police have always been noted for having a flying squad, but not many could boast a flying club, which became a popular leisure activity in our force. One officer who was a DFC was to eventually leave the police and become a pilot with an Indian airline. The other founder member was the watch Inspector at our station. I was talking with someone recently who informed me that it is still thriving. This I find hard to believe with an old Dakota. So next time you see a strange object in the sky it may not be a U.F.O!

All murders have their share of intrigue and mystery, particularly unsolved ones. I recall one in particular. The body of a woman, locally known, was seen by some young boys to be carried from a motor car and deposited in some overgrown bushes. The boys being observant, noted the car's registration number, however there was one snag. They had mixed up the letters creating quite a number of possible permutations. The colour eliminated some, but being a popular colour, left a large number still to be checked. The situation apparently created history because this was the first time a car identification parade had been held. Many drivers were interviewed including a well-liked entertainer, but to my knowledge the murder has never been solved.

There was an almighty bang early one morning, two passenger trains had collided, which obviously caused death and destruction but the part that followed caused much more heartache. Two permanent way workers engaged in clearing up the wreckage, for some reason stepped into the path of a light engine. Perhaps they took a pace back to check their work, or for a break, but the engine hit and killed them both. This was bad enough but the hardest part to cope with was still to come, as both of the workers lived in the same street as the driver. Although he wasn't to blame, it must have been very hard to cope with.

Sometimes the situation leads to sudden changes in a person, mainly due to shock.

One day a Rolls Royce collided with a tree, wiping out three members of a family. Police arrived and inside the vehicle was a very strong smell of alcohol, but the fourth occupant; the driver, who escaped with only minor injuries was stone cold sober. The whole group including the driver had been drinking but in those days the only charges, which could be brought, were manslaughter or driving under the influence of drink or drugs, the latter being the one chosen. The point I am making is how a person can change following a sudden shock and the realisation that he had virtually wiped out his entire family.

On a dark winter's night, I was making a tour of an outlying village. It was wet and windy; I was required to keep a point at the gateway to church. No lights in the street and the entire village had turned in for the night. The Sergeant could turn up and in those days it was a serious offence to miss a point. I thought there's no chance of him coming in this weather. So I snuggled against the wall. All of a sudden I nearly took off, only I couldn't, as I was frozen to the spot. Someone had touched the back of my neck. Regaining my composure I sprang round prepared for anything to discover a friendly cat disappearing along the wall. Had I have caught up with it I wouldn't have been responsible for my actions. Not really, I wouldn't harm any animal, but this one really put the frighteners up me. To cap it all, as I walked to my cycle the Sergeant stepped out of the shadows so my prediction was wrong and by the time I returned to the station, I was a nervous wreck.

I have always enjoyed partaking in sport, particularly football and cricket. It was after a game of football that my career was nearly ended. I contracted a foot virus and was advised that it would not be wise for me to continue as a police officer. I was put on sick leave on a long-term basis, during this period; perhaps somewhat abruptly I resigned. Apart from a little casual work I had little to offer my future wife, so as a last ditch attempt, I applied to join Birmingham City Police and to my utter surprise I was accepted.

Birmingham City Police

My introduction to this force was hectic to say the least. In the morning I was sworn into the city police and in the afternoon I was married.

My wife Margaret and I were treated to the luxury of two days honeymoon in the ancient town of Stafford, before I was sent on a refresher course.

This was far removed from our planned fortnight at the Grand Esplanade Hotel in Jersey.

I had no choice; I was detailed to attend a two weeks course at Mill Meece Police Training Centre.

Obviously this was not the ideal way to cement a marriage, however she was then and remains an absolute brick. Throughout our entire marriage she has been a pillar of strength. Why I don't know, because I don't deserve it. Continually I have been full of crazy ideas, selfish changes, often in the wrong direction. I think that I have slowed down now but I owe her much more than I can ever repay. The weekend flew past which meant a rapid return to reality.

My wife was accommodated in a little village nearby and for me a return to the barrack-room style of life, but only for a short while.

On the first evening a colleague kindly agreed to transport me on his motorcycle to visit my new wife, but it nearly became a very short marriage because we both came off. Why, I'm not sure, maybe I leaned the wrong way or maybe he made a mistake. The only casualty was the turn up of my wedding suit. Someone was smiling at us that night and it just wasn't our turn to go.

After this fortnights course you would have thought that they would have turned me lose on the streets, to make some use of my practical experience, but not likely! Another course, this time on local by-laws. Local by-laws however were extremely useful particularly the power to stop, search, seize and detain with reasonable suspicion. For example if you knew a shop had been broken into at 1.00 am and at 2.00 am you saw a man emerge from a side street carrying a bag, then it would be reasonable to assume that he could be the offender.

Another interesting byelaw that had never been repealed, was aimed at the police officer that failed to arrive on night duty, perhaps through too many beers, could be taken before the magistrate to answer. This was obviously without reasonable excuse.

To my knowledge this was never used however, I conjure up a picture of a ruddy-faced beer-drinking constable being brought before the magistrate to explain his actions. After my training I was posted to the city centre's busy Steelhouse Lane.

The duties were not as wide or varied as those of a county copper, who could deal with a wide range of police work, from issuing movement orders to murders. This was not so in a city, because each area had specialists dealing with whatever occurred. For example, a crime was passed to CID, a sudden death to the Coroners Department, a road traffic accident to the Traffic Department and so on.

So all beat policeman were in effect night watchmen, shaking hands with door knobs by night and a traffic warden by day, sticking foul tasting brown paper onto car tyres along entire streets, with time date and car registration numbers. The idea which didn't always work, was that if the person denied being there for the full length of time, saying that he had been away and returned, then the tyre imprint should be on the brown paper. I hold no grudge against night watchmen or traffic wardens, both of which do an excellent job. It's just that I wasn't cut out for either.

Finding an insecure property often has a strange result, for example, as I tried a hairdressing saloon one night the door opened and there on the floor was a couple. I found them to be the shop manager and his secretary in an extremely compromising position. I am unsure who was the most embarrassed, the couple on the floor or myself, but finding that he was the owner, I beat a hasty retreat and he equally hastily locked the door. I don't think he was prepared to host anymore boys in blue that night!

One late evening I heard a noise in a shop doorway. Thinking I had caught someone breaking in, I crept up to find an old, 'Lady of the road,' taking a huge pinch of snuff, funny old-world! Still, it helped to break up the monotony.

There is a serious side; a very serious side and often incidents are fraught with danger. With hindsight I saw the danger but at the time I just entered into the situation on impulse. Amongst the many situations I recall, was of an intruder in the premises who had made his way onto the rooftops. Two of us climbed a fire escape and by torchlight spotted a figure on the roof, he ran, obviously knowing his way. Giving chase, my torch failed but I carried on only to be struck on the shoulder and thrown back. We lost the man who vanished across the rooftops, checking at what I thought was an object being thrown was found to be telephone wires stretched across the roof. I was extremely grateful because they saved me from plunging into probable oblivion.

I passed the shop on many occasions afterwards and shuddered to think what could have been! Later, after his arrest, it transpired that the man had been a handyman, employed by the shop so no wonder he knew his way around. One certain fact is, I didn't!

One senior member of the legal profession parked his car in a restricted area for a week. During which observations were maintained both day and night. This was one case that he lost, as the stipendiary magistrate calculated his fine by the hour, taking into account, the amount of hours spent by police, keeping an overnight and round the clock vigil. I feel that the case wouldn't have stood a chance in this day and age.

When shifts changed, the incoming officers were paraded, inspected and given information of the days events. One day the Watch Inspector, who we affectionately called 'The Admiral' was relaying this information. Unfortunately he had a nasal problem and talked through his nose, He read, 'Stolen during the night from the Cathedral the Episcopal ring of the bishop.' In reply one of our congregation retorted, "I'll bet he's sore." A comment not appreciated by the Duty Stick, as he was known. I know who it was and it wasn't me. The secret is safe despite the fact that both have retired and probably departed this World.

In a lighter vein, police were often required to show presence at big functions to look after parking etc. This particular evening we were covering a jeweller's ball. I was working with a uniformed Sergeant and during the evening we were approached by a celebrity. The celebrity asked us to call up the owner of a certain car, a Rolls Royce and tell him that he was illegally parked. For doing this he offered us a fiver each. "It's only a practical joke" he said, "He will take it in good part." We declined his offer and at the end of the ball the owners returned to their respective cars. The owner of this one returned and we discovered that he was none other than the Lord Chief Justice of England.

I dread to think of the joke he would have played upon on us, probably still incarcerated in the tower.

Sometimes seemingly safe situations end tragically. One afternoon we went out to our respective areas and this young policeman, being helpful, decided to help a lorry reverse out of the rear of shop premises. This turned out to be the last job he ever did, as he was crushed by the lorry dying instantly. Seems unfair that life sometimes reacts this way.

A common incident at night, to cap the evening's entertainment, was of the drunks being evicted and a drunken scrap-taking place. Many were the time that bodies came flying down the back stairs of one particular pub. If the officer arrested someone, who was then charged, he would be required to appear before magistrates the following day. The officer would also have to give evidence, so would be sent off duty at 2.00 am. Hence a familiar phrase, 'You'll do off at two.' Well at least until this was repeated to the court by one particular gentleman, who obviously wasn't as drunk as we thought. The case was dismissed and the officer finished up getting a rocket from the chairman of the bench. From then onwards our lips were sealed. Much time was wasted hanging around the courts waiting to give evidence. Valuable time, which could have been put too more practical use, like policing the City.

28

Judges had to travel unimpeded from their place of residence, to the Court of Assize, or so the plan was. At each junction a police officer was posted to enable this to happen. Ideally with a front and rear police escort, the sombre procession would make its way along the planned out route. Easy so the planner thought, until one day a young officer decided to let a furniture van reverse out into their path causing, well just a little chaos.

Sometimes, the whole set up became monotonous and for this I volunteered to do the night duty, receiving bodies into the central mortuary. Funeral companies now handle this unenviable task, but at this time it was the police forces responsibility. If there were no bodies, then you assisted the cook.

If a body was brought in, it became our responsibility to organise a search and locate it, ensuring next of kin were informed.

If it were a case of murder, then a Home Office pathologist would be called in to conduct an autopsy. These specialists were brilliant in what they could discover just by a quick examination. For example, the type of weapon used, possible build of an assailant, whether it was committed by a left or right handed person, the probable sex of the attacker, colour of hair, tissue or clothing fibres and blood groups. All the while building up a picture of the person, and helping to secure a conviction. Also whether the attack was sexually motivated.

Mostly however, the deaths were from natural causes, as a result of accidents on the road, at work or in the home.

Sometimes they caused upset, although most of the time you tried to keep an open mind. It was the sort of job that if you let it, could break you up quite quickly.

I recall one particular Christmas Eve at about 10.30 pm I received the body of a small boy. He was as all little ones, very excited about Christmas, but the only difference was, that his heart was weaker than most children, it became too much. I wondered where our maker was that day; perhaps he had better things lined up for him. Only four, I sobbed uncontrollably and I'm not ashamed to say it.

The searching of a body is all-important, particularly if you had a distraction such as this during the same evening.

A body of an elderly bookmaker was brought in, he had been removed from his earthly home whilst in his favourite haunt, a public house. As he was taken into the receiving room, his escort told me not to search him because they had done so, presenting a box containing all or at least they said all of his property. They said that as it was Christmas, they were in a rush to get away and it would save me a job. However, something said that all was not as it appeared. Much to their disgust I carried out a further search during which, I discovered a body belt containing a further £500, a lot of money in the fifties. The escort expressed surprise, but I still had a nasty feeling that someone knew of its existence besides me.

One thing was certain Tommy, the deceased, had taken his last bet. Guess what the first thing the son asked for? His money belt.

In police work, sometimes detection was down to clever and astute detective work, *but luck also played a big part. Being in the right place at the right time. A classic example was when colleagues nipped down a dark entry for a quick smoke, which resulted in a burglar, not only handing his spoils down, but also jumping into the welcoming arms of the law. Not good police work but sheer good luck.

One of the biggest problems in a large City even in those days was the intense volume of traffic, much of our work revolved around ensuring its free flow. The only day traffic was light was on a Wednesday, when under the old shop system 'half day closing' took place, this made the City streets relatively quiet.

It was on one of those Wednesday's that I was window shopping, only gazing idly, I checked the road and started to cross, only having to jump to safety. An extremely irate driver of a Land Rover questioned my pedigree, shouting for me to watch where I was going. He shot off down the street only to be stopped by my colleague, who politely explained to him that he had travelled the wrong way along a one way street. It cost him but I think that was judgement.

We also covered two other police stations, one still in the centre of the City, but the other on the outskirts, the latter being in a fairly rough area. Crime was rife, especially burglaries and was not unusual until it reversed trends. At the start of the night shift we had six officers patrolling, but half way through the night we only had four. The staff manning levels went down by four at end of the shift. A group had been what we called burgling their own beat, by using skeleton keys to enter lock up properties, to steal over quite a period of time. Senior staff were observing their movements and eventually caught two of them red handed. It wasn't

---

* See illustration five "Luck played a big part"

too long before two others were in custody by courtesy of information given. All four received fairly hefty sentences of imprisonment, but the stigma remained for sometime with all of us. Once type cast it was hard to shake off.

Youngsters were often the culprits and some of their tricks needed to be seen to be believed. One I recall happened during the summer holidays. As I turned the street corner I saw a number of children throwing stones at the windows of an unoccupied factory. They did not see me approach, until I was standing directly behind them. It was then too late. I was about to issue a warning to them when the youngsters tried to run off. I stopped one of them where upon he said, *"I didn't paint no car mister," looking quickly around them I saw they were covered in blue paint. I said, "Who did" to which he implicated his big brother. I bade them to show me and they proudly led me to a street near by, pointing to a black Austin motorcar. It displayed more than its fair share of blue paint on tyres,' headlights and bumpers. I'm sure the owner was going to be highly delighted. I was later going to encounter the responsible party in my prison service career and I'm afraid that he was much worse.

Whilst talking of stone throwing episodes, I recall once taking a young officer around to show him the ropes. We passed a group of small boys who he started to make a fuss of. I warned him against this, but to his peril he just ignored me. As we continued on our way he was telling me that I was wrong and they were just normal nice children. Then a stone hit the back of his helmet and three little figures swiftly vanished from sight. Nice little boys eh!

Domestics disputes are to be avoided we were told and this is good advice. I recall entering on several occasions to mediate between spouses, only to find myself as the scapegoat, not only by the aggressor but also ending up on my back, courtesy of the complainant.

During peak periods we were posted to traffic black spots, manning either lights or pedestrian crossings. This particular morning one of the superintendents, a stickler for discipline, walked past whilst I was allowing pedestrians to cross the road. He expected a salute, but both of my arms were engaged holding up traffic. He glared at me as if to say, 'Salute,' still walking and turning his head in my direction, but instead of a salute from me, he ran slap-bang into a lamppost. However I do not

---

* See illustration six "I didn't paint any car mister"

think this was the type of salute he was expecting.

You get used to all the strange sights in a City, including the embarrassing ones. One outstanding one happened around pub and cinema throwing out times. I was quietly patrolling my beat, when walking towards me came three young girls, obviously the worst for wear, as each one was displaying more than enough of next weeks washing, with skirts held high. My dilemma was, do I pretend not to notice and walk past, or if not, what action do I take? Quite a number of people had gathered, so I was forced into action. Fortunately a taxi was passing by so with my best stop signal I brought it to a halt. After a struggle and with the help of a passer by we bundled them into the back seats and away. Phew! All in a night's work! We only had a Belisha Beacon, no radios and trying to run them in for being drunk could have caused enormous problems, especially with three young ladies.

Talking of drunks and modes of transport. One of my colleagues, a short stocky officer, who probably only just made the height limit, was patrolling with a young constable. A woman emerged from a pub obviously hopelessly drunk, staggering and pushing a pram containing a baby. The police station was quite a distance away and the woman had committed an offence. *Quickly thinking, he removed the baby from the pram handed it to the young officer, deposited the woman onto the pram, and carried on pushing the pram towards the police station. This is one of the many situations a policeman is faced with and has to think quickly. Of course his solution may be the wrong one and he could be in trouble for it, but the public expect action and in this case got it. There were no kickbacks from management but plenty of mickey taking from his colleagues.

One night duty, we were all happily eating supper, when the duty inspector walked in looking very glum. We soon understood why, one patrol car crew, covering the areas whilst we were having our break, approached traffic lights on green, had been struck broadside by a car crossing the lights on red and both the driver and observer were very badly injured. No one felt like eating anymore that evening.

Whilst talking of such incidents, none of us will ever forget the bravery of not a policeman, but a member of the public. I have made a

---

* See illustration seven "Quickly thinking he handed the baby to the young officer and deposited the woman in the pram"

policy of not naming anyone in my book, but I will break that rule now. This mans name was Mr Bache. He was travelling on a bus when he saw a scuffle taking place on the pavement, looking again he realised it was a uniformed police officer in trouble. Mr Bache stopped the bus and ran to help him. In the fight he was thrown to the floor, banging his head. Unfortunately he had an eggshell skull and his efforts cost him his life. Mr.Bache was hailed a hero and to all intents and purposes was treated as a police officer, dying in the line of duty. He received a service funeral. We held a collection, and a fund was set up in his memory. Nothing whatsoever would compensate for his loss of life. It left a very nasty taste in our mouths for a long time afterwards and despite the fact that forty years have passed, the incident is one I will never forget, as the police officer he died for, could just as easily have been me.

EXCUSE MADAM, BUT

Store Detective

They say that a change is as good as a rest, so still remaining in law and order, I took a sideways move.

It all happened at a time when I was totally fed up with the monotonous tasks by day as a traffic warden, and by night as a night watchman. Not that I hold anything against either, as both do an equally good job, but it was not the job for me.

I was standing outside a large departmental store, knowing the watchman; he invited me in for a welcomed cuppa. I was moaning about my job and he mentioned the fact that the security supervisor was leaving. This was a posh title for a store detective. Anyway one thing led to another and before I knew it, I had been accepted for the job.

I would not have missed the experience, but it didn't offer the same security or afford the same protection as that of a policeman.

Powers of arrest were restricted to Citizens powers under common law, so if you were making an arrest you had to be absolutely certain of your facts. Wrongful arrest could cost a fortune, and I am sure that the company would not have backed me up should things have gone wrong.

I reported for my first day and was met by my new boss. I felt that I was not over welcome and viewed somewhat suspiciously. He was a legend in the City and feared by many. A scruffy looking man in a dirty old gaberdine raincoat and a cloth cap. He was reputed to have a nose for criminals, I know one thing he did have a nose for, snuff taking, and his clothes bore full evidence of this.

He informed me that my job was to look like a customer by blending in with them. I still had the old coppers measured walk. I was six feet tall and size twelve's. I thought 'blend in' I'd more likely stick out like a sore thumb or foot! He continued to tell me to watch out for criminals, not only shoplifters but staff as well. "Don't get too friendly, as those you get friendly with, may well be on the fiddle."

He explained the calling system. If we are required, two coloured lights will appear on the bank of lights above all lifts on each floor; ours was red and amber. There were no means of radio communication in those days, so assistance was slow to arrive.

He warned of certain tell tale signs, such as people making furtive glances i.e. looking sharply around them, he demonstrated. "Watch their eyes and fidgety fingers" but the one, which baffled me, was of elderly women singing to themselves usually after four in the afternoon. His tips were invaluable and usually right.

So armed with these valuable snippets of information I was told to work alone, covering the ground and basement floors. They held a wide a range of goods, including tools, china, food, haberdashery, perfumes, cosmetics and stationary.

Setting out on my new job I decided that I should introduce myself to the various floor managers. So setting out on the ground floor. I walked towards the manager's office when something caught my eye.

A well-dressed man standing alongside a display opened up a briefcase and quickly deposited two articles into it. I couldn't believe my eyes. Still watching him, I sidled to an internal phone, and gave instructions for the lights for calling support to be switched on. This happened immediately and within minutes, assistance arrived in the form of my boss. I explained to him what I had seen, but he just shook his head, taking my arm he completely astounded me. This by walking directly up to the man and saying "May I introduce you to the General Manager."

"Never mind" he said almost sympathetically "They'll come along soon, and you'll have more than you want before your know it." Again he was right.

Children were very vulnerable and telegraphed their intentions well in advance of the act.

Secretly I felt sorry for many, because they were sent into town, given a few shillings and told not to come back until tea-time.

So what happened? Into town they came, found a shop selling ice cream or sweets, spent their money and still had many hours to wait before returning home. Then starts the wondering, eventually finding a big departmental store where they play, pester or steal, often the latter.

Most people would blame the parents, and I agree to some extent, but not entirely! Part of the blame lies with the stores themselves. Brightly lit open counters, inviting kids to have a go. No one will see, but unfortunately they do. Kids were so easy to catch, but who really wanted to label them a criminal before they had even started to grow up.

It was just before Christmas. The toy department was full of bright attractive toys, for those who could afford them, some however couldn't and tried other ways. One of the displays was a full layout of a railway track with trains that toed and froed quite happily. Light engines, goods trains, passenger trains, stopping and starting, entering and emerging from tunnels. It certainly held my attention, also the attention of a small lad in a macintosh about three times too big for him. The assistant on the other hand was more attracted to a group of male assistant's busily engaged in conversation, certainly not paying any attention to the display. The boy eyed me suspiciously, so I wandered off behind a panel at the side. He gave me a quick look, as a light engine emerged from the tunnel so it vanished up his sleeve and off he ran. I gave chase, caught him and returned him to the office. At first he denied the theft, but when I told him what I had seen he produced it. I hadn't the heart to take it all the way, so I gave him a very sound talking to and warned him of a fate worse than death should I ever see him again, then sent him packing.

I returned to the department and confronted a rather arrogant manager, who emphatically denied having lost anything. I pointed to the display where the assistant was still talking, and then to the manager's astonishment I produced the engine. I respectfully suggested that maybe if his staff paid more attention to their job, rather than to the boys, then the company might lose less merchandise.

As for the little boy, I doubted if this would be the only time he would fall foul of the law, but at least he had not been left with a criminal tag too early in his life.

One character I encountered always wore a bright yellow cravat with horseshoes on it. He was a well-known shoplifter and had many previous convictions, he was no stranger to prison, and I was to meet him later in my main career. We were never able to catch him, but his explanations given to me, as a prison officer sum it all up.

You could not make an arrest until the person had actually left the store, and even then you would chose your words very carefully indeed, for fear of being wrong.

A classic example of this, which sticks in my mind to this day, was when I was keeping my eye on the basement. When pondering whether to go for coffee, I clearly saw an elderly lady remove a tin of paint from a display counter and put it into a carrier, move over to another counter and repeat the act on two other occasions. Suddenly, she ran up the staircase closely pursued by myself. Catching up with her I said "Excuse me but I think that you have something which you have forgotten to pay for." She said, "No I'm just running to catch my bus." I explained to her exactly what I had seen. Confident of my ground I felt that she was stalling for time. Fortunately for me she was a very reasonable person replying "Let me show you something." She removed the tins from her bag, producing them saying "Take hold." I did so, and found only empty tins. "There you are" she then went on to explain that she was the wife of a farmer and they had been decorating their house. During the weekend they had run out of three types of paint, and she had travelled in to try to buy replacements. Having no luck she suddenly realised that if she did not hurry, she would miss her bus. I apologised, and then made myself conspicuous by my absence. I never saw her again. I did learn object lessons from this event.

The first being 'Don't jump to conclusions' and secondly 'Don't believe all you that you see, or what it first appears to be'.

Thinking back I should have known because of the speed at which she tackled the steps. Had the tins have been full, she wouldn't have been able to move so quickly.

The more blatant the thief, I found, the more chance he had of getting away with his crime.

One man, who entered the store, made his way to the hand luggage department, stole a travel bag and casually walked round the store filling it with other stolen articles. Much had been taken, including several large items.

Each morning we had a briefing and amongst other things, this was one topic mentioned. Later that day he turned up, and true to form, helped himself to a travel bag and began to fill it with stolen goods. This was not a time to be tactful, we just had to grab him directly as he left the building, otherwise he would be away like a rocket. We converged on him and eventually apprehended him. In the ensuing struggle a number of cards fell onto the floor, we discovered that these were left luggage tickets for the main Birmingham railway stations. Many items were recovered by police including a heater and a small chair. As he stole, so he stored.

He appeared before the court pleading guilty, but his counsel put forward a plea mitigating his actions. Apparently he was a redundant car worker who, had been prescribed a course of anti-depressant drugs. According to his counsel, the drugs could have side effects, such as wanton theft. He called medical evidence to support this claim. I found this a bit hard to swallow, pardon the pun. He was eventually put on probation.

Another blatant act to further illustrate the point occurred when, a man dressed in an overall with our company motif on the pocket, entered the building one morning just as staff was beginning to arrive. He made his way to the floor selling ladies coats, approached an assistant and asked for the manager. The assistant without thinking explained that the manager hadn't arrived. He produced an invoice explaining that a consignment of furs had been delivered incorrectly and he had to collect them, however as the manager had not arrived, he would wait. The girl said she didn't see any reason why he couldn't take them. This was the opportunity he was waiting for, and he loaded the mobile rail with a number of furs and left the building never to be seen again. He was of course a thief who had pulled a very blatant and clever theft. The invoices of course were fictitious, the assistant believing they were real, allowed him to remove them. The only way she could have been sure was by asking for verification at his depot and may be, just may be, the ruse would have been uncovered.

Not all store detectives work was confined to shoplifting. They dealt with many aspects of detective work, amongst which, was with staff. A very watchful eye was called for, especially amongst those who had direct access to tills.

There were a number of ways by which assistants would try to 'ring the changes'. Margins of error were allowed for. This was another occasion when the boss gave sound advice, however when listening to it, I thought, "What the dickens is he talking about." One was, whilst having a coffee, watch out for any assistant smoking a Black Russian cigarette, particularly young staff spending heavily. They were not paid sufficiently to warrant a smoke of such luxury. Again this proved to be true on numerous occasions. Strangely enough, once confronted they would admit it straight away, as though they were waiting to get caught, and now they had been, seemed relieved.

A 'No Sale' rung up on the till, would also give an indication of theft taking place, also, the ringing up of reduced amounts as per each transaction. IE a sale of £13, ringing up £10 and keeping the difference. If approached, staff would usually admit to an error. It wasn't good policy to act instantly, it was better for them to be watched, over a period of time, and it was for this purpose, we employed a special company to make test purchases over a given period.

The company, an Australian one, operated on a secret basis, not even we knew whom they were, but they constantly came up with excellent results. Should any staff have been allowed to get away with it, the cost to the company would have been great. Many staff could well work, in the same day, on a number of tills, however the methods of deceit were carefully noted. The resulting action was dismissal.

Staff were allowed to purchase items at reduced prices, but some, were not satisfied with these discounts. They would hand in goods to the staff purchase department, say a pound of cod on the ticket, but closer examination would reveal double, or even treble the quantity, not of cod, but fresh salmon. The same trick would be tried out with cheap cuts of meat, which would turn out to be best cuts of steak. I felt that the firm suffered a considerable loss by this method of theft. Malpractices weren't restricted only to food, clothing, perfume, china were all shown at marked down prices. We didn't catch them all, but when we caught someone, it quietened the others down for a time.

Each night, door staff would tear the tickets off the appropriate staff packages; often this would just be a perfunctory gesture of little meaning. So on occasions we used to converge, checking every ones bags and packages. Who better to set a good example in front of his staff than one of very senior management, as he approached he was requested to open his brief case? He appeared angry, but being perfectly within our rights he complied, albeit somewhat reluctantly. We understood the reason why, as all it contained were cheese sandwiches and a set of darts.

An absolute nightmare to a store detective is the 'dip,' a purse thief and pickpocket. Dips dipped into shopping bags, which had exposed purses and wallets. A very common habit with many people, thus giving the crook the very opportunistic chance he has been waiting for.

If someone in a crowd yelled out, "Watch out there's a pick-pocket about," then the most likely people yelling, would be the thieves themselves, the automatic reaction to this statement would be for shoppers to check their wallets and purses. This gave the thief a clear indication of exactly where a person's purse or wallet was located.

On a bad afternoon anything up to twenty purses or wallets have vanished. Usually these offences would happen on Saturday.

The nightmare comes, when a gang arrives and becomes immediately busy, searching with their eyes quickly darting from person to person. A gang would consist of around eight members, but only two would probably be operating, with the other six acting as decoys. The six would split into pairs or even alone and wander all over the stores five levels, making all the moves we would be looking for in this type of criminal.

At times such as these, we would borrow detectives from both the police and other stores. Pickpockets move very rapidly and are extremely tiring to follow. If you found one and decided to follow, you just dare not to let them go. Sometimes the trail would move to other towns and very often finish in a fight.

To successfully make an arrest would give a great sense of achievement, but very often it would be a wild goose chase with nothing at the end.

My tip to anyone carrying a purse or wallet is to carry it on a sensitive part of your body so, if anyone tries to steal it, you become immediately aware that someone is intruding into your personal space.

It was a gorgeous morning, one that made me feel glad to be alive, at least that is how it started, however not for everyone.

As I walked onto the fashion floor, I was approached and shown an open window leading onto a parapet. Normally I hate heights, but I clambered out to where a figure was standing on the corner of the building. Unfortunately before she was reached, she jumped, plunging down and striking a road sign. I don't know how I got back to the window, but I did, only to learn that she had died. I felt sad, it apparently was her birthday but instead of celebrating she decided to end it. I inwardly blamed myself, but there was little more that I could have done. When someone is as determined as she was, it proves very difficult to sway his or her mind.

There was a vast variety of incidents, not least of which, were sex offenders. I suppose that the era was partly to blame, as it was the time of the mini skirt and the extra exposure of female attributes.

One man used to go into the basement and drop coins on the floor, whilst recovering the money, he would cast his eyes upwards and look up young ladies skirts as they climbed the stairs. There was no proof of any offence and without a complaint it was difficult to act, however there was one thing in our favour, this being the 'ways and means' act.

My boss thought for a while then collected a number of empty boxes to form a barricade. We secreted ourselves and waited. I was somewhat mystified, for he was clutching a large brown paper bag. As usual I posed no question, as he was the master of his trade.

True to form the pervert arrived, dropping his coins and proceeded to look up. This time however he got more than an eyeful, with precision timing my boss burst open the bag. An ugly brown cloud appeared and drifted slowly on top of the peeper, a brief pause, then a sudden violent outburst of sneezing, and the peeper left the store at a fair rate of knots, never to be seen again.

My boss burst into fits of laughter, 'Pepper Jim' I enquired, 'No snuff' he replied still laughing as we walked off.

The job variety is what made it so interesting however; it did not always produce success.

The old fellow who used to wear a yellow cravat studded with horses hoofs and riding crops was a classic example. Every act he carried out would appear to be an act of theft, but many times he would return the article to its rightful position before meddling with something else. Most of the items were menswear, but we never seemed to catch him 'bang to rights." Occasionally he was caught and paid the ultimate penalty of imprisonment. It was whilst in the Prison Service I discovered the reason of his actions.

Imagine his and my surprise when he was one of my first charges on the landings upon joining the prison service. "Aren't you bloody well satisfied in putting me here, without following me as well," that was his comment. He was a likeable character and we got to know each other well. One day I enquired of him, why he carried out the actions he had and never stole anything. He began to go into graphic detail of his actions, explaining how he used to deliberately fold an item, and go through the motions of secreting them in his coat pockets. Then just return the item and wander off to another area, to perform to the same act all over again.

"I knew all of you" he said "But what you didn't know was, my wife was on the other floors with no one watching her, as you were all to busy watching me."

What a blow, I felt that we had been hoodwinked, and we had. Unfortunately once discharged, he fell down the steps of a city store, meeting his end. So the secrets I discovered were taken with him to his grave.

Some shoplifters would walk into a changing room, emerging in a complete change of clothes.

One afternoon we were alerted by an assistant on the ladies floor who was convinced that a woman had stolen several pairs of panties. After detaining her, my boss told her that she had stolen the items. He was on safe ground because she was a well-known shoplifter. As cool as ice, she hiked up her skirt and removed six pairs of panties. I don't know who was the most embarrassed, my boss or I, as I felt myself turning a nice shade of crimson, and could feel my ears burning.

Staff, even management, carried out sometimes-clever frauds. I remember a big fraud being carried out by a carpet departmental manager. It took place on a half-day closing. At this time the company used the opportunity to deliver goods. The carpet department being no exception. Many of the goods were delivered by off duty fireman to various addresses around the Birmingham area.

At this time deficiencies were noticed and an investigation was carried out. It revealed that the delivery recipients were contacts of a certain manager, the accompanying invoices being fictitious. Once delivered the manager would collect the orders from the various addresses. A case was presented; he was duly charged and appeared before a court, where he received an eighteen-month sentence of imprisonment. Another use for carpets not exactly, as intended, was a muffle for a safe blower. He carried out his crime during the night after apparently secreting himself on the premises. It was impossible for him to be discovered in such a vast building. It would have been by sheer good fortune if someone had found him.

He got away, after blowing the safe in the strong room, but his freedom was short lived and for his pains, received seven years imprisonment. I was to discover later, that the criminal fraternity considers prison terms, to be mere occupational hazards.

Once an intruder was suspected of being on the premises, so a police dog and its handler carried out a search. The dog began his search and much to its handler's horror, began to cock his leg up an armchair, rather than search. He was called back and given a good telling off for his sin, when a wet bedraggled man emerged. Not only had the dog achieved satisfying his needs, but had also done what he was sent to do, by effecting an arrest.

Occasionally we would have to work nights especially when outside contractors were working. One time it was the escalator service engineer. Throughout the night he flitted to and from the area where he was supposed to be, to where his van was located, on the pretext of collecting tools. However this was not his intention, as each time he went to his vehicle, he also deposited an item of clothing. Perhaps if his journeys had been less frequent, we would not have become suspicious, but as it was, the police search revealed a large amount of menswear. This was one occasion when being blatant didn't pay.

I have tried to outline some of the cases that cropped up in this field and explained some of the methods used.

I have however seen many others, for example. Using a baby as cover for what the hands are doing, placing a carrier on the wrist and using fingers to manipulate goods into the bag whilst, at the same time looking at another item with the other hand. This is a very hard one to see, and then you are not sure whether or not you are imagining things. People would take items they had no need for, or could easily have paid for. Some would steal, slightly damage the item, and return it for a refund at a later date. Some would collaborate with staff or use the accomplice as a decoy.

Once a man was using both his baby and his wife for cover by distraction, they held the baby close to where the thefts were being committed to cover his actions. Inevitably greed leads to false confidence, and eventually they were caught. Unfortunately he was a police officer, who had fallen on hard times through gambling, and was stealing to pay off his debts. A career thrown away because of greed.

Shoplifting is said to be a disease called kleptomania, but now days it is a big business. In my time of working in this field, I came to blame the lure and openness of displays. Bright lights all spelling out 'Come and help yourself, its easy.' The various types of thief knew no bounds and ranged from little children to professional people.

Stores are now working together to combat crime. In towns and cities each member of various schemes has radio contact with other stores. If known shoplifters are around, they can be targeted and their movements carefully monitored. In addition, each has photo albums of the criminals. However I don't think that shoplifting will ever be completely obliterated, despite the uniformed guards and the sophisticated security equipment. There will always remain, people who despite the odds stacked against them, try to beat the system and cannot resist the challenge offered to them.

LEARNING THE TRICKS OF THE TRADE

The Mystery Unfolds

To the majority of us, prisons are a mystery. All we see from outside, are forbidding looking buildings surrounded by high walls. The only information we glean is from the media. Not always a true picture.

Before I take you into this world, I will try to make some comparisons in an effort to give a clearer picture to those you, who are as mystified as I was.

I see prisons as small self-contained towns, operating their own systems of administration and control. For this purpose, I make a comparison with any town, whose control is effected by a Council, headed by a leader, Not too much different from a prison governing body which, instead of a Council, has what is known as a 'Board of Visitors.' This is headed by a chairperson instead of a leader. This board meets at frequent intervals, discussing the prisons legislation and policy. Hearing any complaints made either by prisoners or indeed staff, both of who may see either a single member, or the full board. Similar to the so-called surgeries held by Councillors.

Members of the board are elected and approved by the Secretary of State. The criteria are, that they must not have any pecuniary business interest involving the prison, and are of good character.

They have additional responsibilities which, are to sit and hear adjudication's for offences committed by prisoners of the more serious nature. For example, riotous behaviour, escaping or serious assaults. For this reason a certain number must be qualified as justices of the Peace.

Normal day to day adjudication's of a less serious nature, are heard and dealt with by the prison Governor. I will deal with these in more detail at a later stage. Again this is similar to the two-tier system of crown and magistrates courts.

As with a town, a prison caters for all forms of religious belief, many have churches and resident ministers for the major religions. Hospitals are built into most large prisons with resident medical staff available, including, consultants and surgical facilities. At some prisons, factories and workshops provide employment, producing goods for use mainly within the prison itself. Trained staff operates laundries and dry cleaning facilities and in some prisons there are internal labour exchanges. The local authority provides libraries, these being operated by staff from the library service. Qualified teachers offer educational facilities. Fitness centres comparable to health clubs with qualified instructors are available. Maintenance is self contained, policed by prison officers with higher ranks supervising, eventually rising to prison governor who represents an equivalent grade to Chief Constable.

So as you can see they operate not unlike a small town. One problem that they do not have, which all towns do, is that of parking. Still with all the changes in control and more liberal policies, who knows!

If you view this section with this in mind, it may help you to follow more clearly the prison system.

Joining the Service

After a while, being a store detective didn't seem to be so attractive and the error of my hasty decision began to feature clearly in my mind. I needed more stability and security, for the future and permanency of my current work could not be guaranteed.

So again I went on the search. It couldn't be the police, because I had had enough chances, but I wanted something of a similar nature. I looked at a whole range of options, coupled with a book I had recently read entitled 'Prison Governor,' I decided to give the prison service a try. So without much a do I sent for details. The brochure gave me an insight into the work, which appealed to me so I sent my application in post haste.

The only fear I held was that of capital punishment, and having to be present, as this was part of the services responsibility. I didn't need to worry for long, as not long into my service it was abolished. I did however supervise a number of prisoners who received this sentence, which I will describe later.

I completed my application to join the service by return of post, but I needn't have bothered to rush, as I was to find the wheels of the Home Office grind very slowly. Ages later I received a reply inviting me to attend for tests.

My initial reaction on approaching Stafford Prison was to turn round and go home, but common sense prevailed and I knocked. The greeting I received was far from welcoming. The big plump man who opened the door must have thought I was a prisoner, until I explained. His remark was "Another mug." I was beckoned into a waiting room that seemed bereft of any mod cons. Shortly afterwards, my escort arrived to take me to another room, here I had to sit tests on Maths, English and general knowledge. This was not too difficult. After passing the tests, I moved to the next stage, a medical, which was much stricter. Its amazing, the magic worked by running taps when they want a sample of your water! I was told that I had a curved spine, but this would not bar me from selection, I breathed a sigh of relief.

The human side came in and I was taken for a cup of tea. Whilst in the mess I felt very vulnerable. I knew my faults, but I felt as if I was something out of a freak show, according to the strange looks I kept getting. No one seemed to want to speak, despite my efforts.

Tea over, I was taken to the board room, sitting behind the table were three men, this was the interviewing panel and I was to find out it comprised of Governor, Chief Officer and the Steward, now called the Administration Officer.

Questions were fired by all the members of the panel, they delved into my previous careers, enquired why I had left, especially the police. They probed into my family background and presented me with one or two hypothetical problems. They asked what I expected from the service and what I was prepared to give in return. Giving me the opportunity to ask any questions.

They finally warned me that, I would be expected to work, adding "Of course if you are selected," extremely unsociable hours, in extremely unsociable conditions, with very unsociable people. I remember thinking to myself; he must be referring to the staff, if my first impressions were anything to go by.

I left the prison somewhat dejected, drained, and with no decision being made, a feeling that I couldn't care less.

Another long wait, I was thinking about giving up, when I received a letter complete with joining instructions. Report to H M Prison Birmingham on Monday 18th March 1963. My enthusiasm began to return, so fired up, I decided to go for it.

On the appointed day I reported to H M Prison Winson Green. As I approached on this dull March morning, it suddenly loomed up at me. As with most Victorian prisons it was situated in a city suburb, at the side of a busy road.

The enormous collection of buildings were surrounded by a high wall, of about 17ft in height and it appeared endless as it disappeared around corners and continued on its way.

I approached the tall pair of arched wooden gates, took the heavy knocker in my hand, paused and let it go. A small aperture opened the person inside enquired of my business. "I'm starting my training here today," he took my letter and the aperture closed. The knowledge that I was starting training must have worked miracles, because twenty minutes later he decided to let me enter, and see, what was my fist glimpse inside a prison.

The gatekeeper beckoned me into a small waiting room. Whilst waiting and getting my bearings, I noticed a very large pair of iron gates, with sufficient distance between them to accommodate a vehicle. They were known as the outer and inner gates, and as I was to discover later, was where vehicle searches were conducted when vehicles arrived or departed the prison.

Several other men were joining on the same day and slowly they arrived. All of us, somewhat hesitant, at what we had let ourselves in for. In retrospect I'm sure that my choice was the right one.

This time we didn't have a long wait. A plump, ruddy-faced man in uniform introduced himself as the training P.O. In those days he was one of those hallowed ranks that all uniformed staff were expected to salute.

The group of us was taken to an office, gathering strange looks and amused smiles from men attired in grey battledress with blue striped shirts. Our future charges. In the office we were issued with a Prison Service cap badge which; we were to place in our lapel buttonhole.

In addition to this, we each received a notebook which, I was to discover were generally known as "Grassing Books". The object of these books was to enter comments on each day's assignments. Innocently some trainees were entering comments in these books which, exposed some of the malpractice's of their more senior colleagues, an example being 'Reported for landing duty with Officer Bloggs.' 'Went into the kitchen, where we had a bacon sandwich and a cup of tea.' Both of which being illegal, gave the superior officer the information, and the officer showing the trainee the job, a deal of explaining to do. No wonder they viewed us with suspicion and resented our presence. Who could blame them?

We covered the very wide range of officers duties, from unlock to lock up, with mishaps along the way. For example, whilst in reception a group of prisoners awaiting transfer, were milling around just waiting. All were dressed in their own clothes; I was in sports coat and flannels, the only difference was my badge. Suddenly I found myself herded into a large holding cell and the door slammed. I quickly removed my badge and took the stance 'If you can't beat them join them.' Imagine their faces when the cell door was eventually opened and I replaced my badge, no official even missed me!

Another attachment was to attend the visits rooms and observe the procedure. This was where both non-convicted and convicted prisoners received their statutory visits. There was a closed section and a large open room. I was assigned to the open room where I was instructed to stand along the side, I chose to stand alongside some long yellow curtains.

The visits commenced, the tables began to fill, *when all of a sudden the doors burst open and in came a large contingent of staff, led by the Chief Officer. Seeing all was quiet, he directed an icy glare at me. He walked over and using some most uncomplimentary words advised me to move from the wall. This I did, and the alarm bell ceased to ring. I had been leaning on the alarm bell, which was secreted behind the curtain.

I commend the Chief 's command of Anglo-Saxon; he didn't mince, or repeat any words in telling me my fortune. He departed the visits, fixing me with another icy stare. I thought to myself, what a silly place to put an alarm bell. The one thing I did learn was to ensure that I was aware of the exact position of all the alarm buttons, in every building, I entered in the future.

---

* See illustration eight "All of a sudden the doors burst open and in came a large contingent of staff"

The incident took some living down amongst my colleagues, visitors I think felt sorry for me, but I felt a complete idiot!

The idea of the month spent at a prison, before undergoing the full training course, is to ensure that you are suitable to the service and that you get an insight into what lies ahead of you. It is pointless continuing if you feel at all uncomfortable. New staff are given attachments to all posts and work with experienced officers.

They learn how important accountability is and knowing where all their charges are at all times. They learn all aspects of landing duties, as a landing is the prisoner's home for the ensuing months or years.

A day is spent seeing procedures when prisoners are received into prison, or discharged when they have completed their sentence. Another day in the Gate Lodge.

Also you see the prison hospital, the afternoon visits, how the library and the canteen work and many other things besides. You are in the people business and your prize tool is your ability to handle them.

Some attachments leave a lasting impression, particularly when for example you have opened and closed the huge iron gates a few hundred times in a day. Or the uncanny smell associated with morning ablutions of 'slopping out,' as it is known, down wind was definitely the favoured position, particularly if you were gifted with a keen sense of smell.

Another job that left a lasting impression on your feet, was visits runner. This meant that as visitors began to arrive, you had to race around the prison trying to locate each prisoner being visited, easy if they were where they should be, but a nightmare if they were not. However not too many hid, as it was their visiting times. You would just get back with a batch, looking forward to a break, then find yourself with another group to collect from all parts of the prison. I remember one day, I had been particularly busy and the P.O. told me to have a smoke break, for which I was very grateful. No sooner I had lit up and started to unwind, when the P.O. took the cigarette from me and gave me yet another long list. I thought 'Sadist,' this was a job reserved for the dog under the underdog!

Training School

The training school I attended was located in Wakefield. The accommodation being similar to army barrack rooms. The occupants would be our constant companions for eight weeks and would share in our triumphs, heartaches and worries, as indeed we would share in theirs. This was a good policy because, from the start, it taught us the benefits of teamwork and spirit. A very essential quality in a prison officer's make up, many was the time that good teamwork retrieved a difficult or nasty situation.

The course was designed to be a mix of physical and theoretical tuition. For some it was not easy to revert to class work, and for others it wasn't easy to suffer the hardships of the gymnasium, particularly the unfit ones, however clever they may have been.

The course itself, was one where participants could be failed at anytime, without reasons being given as to why! Just simply that the rejects were not considered suitable material to make good prison officers. On our course 154 started and only 72 survived.

Training took the form of two four-week periods, with a break at the fourth week stage. By which time most of the unsuitable had been weeded out, many of whom seemed much better suited to the job than some of us who had survived. It was strange to return from our break to half empty classes. Much emphasis was placed on theory of prison law and procedures. Every item had to be neatly written in our own time, not so nowadays, handouts are issued and all the trainee has to do is file, and learn from them. We however, had at least two hours work each evening, before we could pack up and troop a couple of miles to the local hostelry for a night-cap. Another luxury was the town's fish and chips; both commodities were so cheap and delicious especially being far away from home cooking. Some of the lads thoughts turned to girls, not our little group however, we would head back to our beds to dream of the following days tortures in the gym. HONEST!

PE was divided into two sections. Firstly we had to be able to control and organise group PE activities. Each of us in our turn had to come to the front and take the class. If any one thought they would go easy on their pals, there was no chance! The PE instructor would quickly see through the ruse and make the student instructor tighten up his lesson, which meant we all suffered more in the long run.

Talking of suffering, the second part of PE training was devoted to self-defence. We all had to parade in canvas judo suits and twist each others arms and legs into a various contorted shapes. Many resulted in having to attend hospital, for treatment for injuries sustained whilst practising the movements. Some were badly hurt and finished up being failed medically, to be told that, when they were fit again, they could rejoin another course and complete the remainder of they're training. Many however didn't bother to return. Some joined the police, a much easier option than ours. It was said that failures on the course would be welcomed into Wakefield police.

The selection process was harrowing to say the least; you filed in on the Friday of the fourth week, after breakfast and parade. The instructors ushered some of the group into the main lecture hall, and the others into the common lounge. Neither group knew whether they had passed or failed. I was ushered into the hall and shortly afterwards a lecturer started giving us a lesson. So either by good luck or by good judgement, we were the lucky ones. We never saw the others again.

At the eighth week final stage, they reversed the procedure, so just as we were convinced we had failed, and we were told we had passed. I don't know how the others must have felt, thinking that they had passed.

This system has now changed and potential failures are weeded out before they start training, after which the reminder, are able to relax in the knowledge that unless they do something drastic at the training school, they would not be failed.

A much fairer system in my view as people can concentrate on learning rather than worrying about failure. Each morning we were assembled by each section. One particular morning we were confronted by the Commandant and the Chief Officer who, informed us that some one had taken a washing line of ladies underwear on his way back from the pub, and if they cared to own up nothing more would be said. The man owned up, maybe nothing was said, but plenty was done. The police were waiting. The culprit was charged and dismissed from the course. So much for nothing more being said. This left a nasty taste because of people not keeping their word.

Another time during a lecture, as the tutor swung round, his pointer smashed a lampshade. Someone in the class laughed out loud. He also failed. May be there were other reasons but wasn't it co-incidental. All this created was unnecessary stress. I'm glad to say it has all changed.

It was said that these pressures were put on us to measure our resilience for the future, and whether we could handle a tight situation. I feel this was nonsense as the uncertainty created much stress and being continually in that uncertain condition surely didn't help in absorbing all the information.

During the eight weeks we had to qualify in first aid, Civil defence and marching. To us ex-service men, marching was easy however, can you imagine the difficulty experienced by those non serviceman who, marched swinging their left foot and left arm together followed by the right foot and right arm. These people looked like tin soldiers.

They unfortunately were unable to co-ordinate their movements. It was easy for some to ridicule, but so difficult for them to be able to carry out the correct movements. Fortunately the ex-drill men on the course spent spare time with them, and by the end of the eight weeks they were able to master the drill movements.

I feel that if one experiences hardships, then one is more able to empathise with people in similar situations. This was invaluable when I became a tutor later in my career.

Once my pal and I, for a change had nothing to write, so we decided to visit a village which we discovered had a fun fair. After spending some time there, we returned to my car, which I unlocked and jumped in, my colleague joined me sitting in the passenger seat. I was about to start up the engine and move off, when my passenger said 'I didn't notice that leopard skin cover on your steering wheel before.' I was about to say that I hadn't got one when I went cold. Suddenly realising we were in the wrong car. Imagine explaining the predicament to the police who were out in full strength because of the fun fair. We were glad to skulk out of that car and into our own and away as fast as our little car could carry us. So much for security of car keys.

There were two types of courses held in the Wakefield area. The prison service training, ranging from recruit to Governors, because in Wakefield the prison service staff college was situated, as well as the officers training school.

The other being a detective training school. I am sure that to the locals we all stood out like 'Sore Thumbs'.

On courses of this nature, one tends to let ones hair down when off duty, which was good for trade in the local hostelries. Members of whatever course could be seen converging and working miracles for the licensee's profit. Whilst on the course we learned all the correct procedures, from the initial reception of a prisoner right up until his ultimate discharge. How to handcuff correctly, general court procedures, placing a man on report, landing duties, prisoners entitlements, night patrols, completing documentation etc.

Armed with this knowledge, only to be disillusioned when arriving at our permanent posting, by being told to forget all that we had learned at the school, and adopt the system, which varied from prison to prison. I must say that nothing dampens a keen young officer's spirits more than being given such advice. Some old chiefs made sure that, staff joining after being thoroughly trained, were made to comply with local systems, rather than applying what they had recently been taught at the training centres.

In this day and age there are too many loopholes, and opportunities for prisoners to take out litigation against staff. Thus officers feel very vulnerable and unprotected, therefore more inclined to ignore bad advice such as this, and stick to the rulebook by carrying out correct procedures.

HIGH WALLS AND LOCKED DOORS

In The Green

During our farewell end of course speech, the Commandant remarked that our course was one of the worst courses he ever had encountered. Disillusioned, but relieved to be through, as the Dutch courage built up during the evening one of the lads asked him why?

His reply inferred that the remarks were not directed at us, but towards certain temporary members of the training team, who apparently had been mis-behaving whilst away from home. At least it let us off the hook and we didn't depart with a guilt complex. Only a hangover! My posting was to Birmingham prison.

A repeat performance of the last arrival at the gate. Thinking that as we had got through the training school stage, we would probably receive more civility and be accepted. Not at all, - the same face and the same cryptic remarks, except that he added, "And don't forget everyone is addressed as Sir in here," - "Except for these bastards," indicating a grinning prisoner. I thought to myself, after taking an instant dislike to this officer, "Since when have you been knighted." But in hindsight I made a wise decision, because although I'm tall, he was taller and massively built. Had he decided to clip my ears it was that cold that they would have fallen off. So I took the safest option and buttoned my lip.

All of us met at the gate lodge waiting room. It is said, that the gate officer and the reception officer being the first people met by any one entering, either as a guest or a visitor epitomises the service. Well this one didn't do anything towards fostering good relationships, because we all wished we were miles away. As for me, I wished that I was back in the police, at least I would have been over my sprog days.

A plump, ruddy-faced senior member of staff arrived and informed us that he was the training P.O.

At the time I joined, apart from officer, the grades were Principal Officer and Chief Officer, abbreviated to P.O. and Chief I or II (COI or COII.)

A Chief walked on hallowed ground, and usually, the only time you got into conversation with one was when you were in trouble.

A P.O. was a slightly lower grade, but nevertheless, you were expected to salute him and he wielded a lot of power.

Our training P.O. certainly created a much better impression upon us, and made us feel that we were part of a team and were wanted.

I'm sure that Chief's were human, but at this stage nothing would convince me that this was the case.

A Chief Officer Grade I wore gold braid on his cap, gold chinstraps and epaulettes. So you would think that with all that scrambled egg he wouldn't be hard to detect, but you would be amazed at the number of times he managed to catch us unawares, usually when we were up to mischief. He was the Prison Governor's right hand man, and any matter relating to uniformed staff was his responsibility. He discreetly advised his Governor as to the running of the prison.

The advice given to his Governor, could I think, be termed more as gentle persuasion. Especially in matters relating to operational numbers.

After a brief audience with him we were given a guided tour of the prison. It was huge; I remember thinking it will take me ages to find my way around this place properly.

The residential area can be described as T shaped, with a central point on the ground floor from where everything was controlled by a senior staff member, known as the centre P.O. No one walked across the centre, everyone walked around it. From the centre a spiral iron stairway led to two sets of landings above, and one below, making four levels. From which at each level, three long landings projected forming the shape of a letter T.

Safety wire formed a net stretching the length and breadth of each landing. This netting was in place to prevent suicide attempts, or anyone including staff from being thrown over, coming to a sticky end. Occasionally, we would have to arrest some fool running amok. The sensation can best be described as – Like a trampoline without any spring to it.

When the cleaners swept it, howls of protest came from the floors below, because all the dust found its way onto the ground floor, not fostering particularly good relationships between landing cleaners.

Wings were indicated by a letter i.e. A, B and C, and landings by numbers working from the bottom upwards ie.1, 2,3,4. One being the floor below ground level and four top of the shop.

Continuing on our tour we visited the other wings. The first held mainly first timers, known as stars, because they wore a red star on the sleeve of their jackets and occupied the top two landings. The idea was to keep them segregated from those known as recidivists, 'American word for repeaters,' meaning people who keep returning to prison. It was thought that the regulars would lead the others into their bad habits. Personally I didn't see this as being true, in fact, a fair proportion of stars were convicted murderers, and many had graduated from borstal boys to adult prisoners. So in effect, they were as worldly wise as many of those classed as recidivists.

The bottom two landings were occupied by the prisons hospital patients and people detained for mental or medical observations. Some strange people! One such patient would drink tea from his plastic chamber pot and use his mug to urinate in.

Another would walk around mimicking farm animals. And yet another would imagine himself as a great singer and alternatively as a punch-drunk boxer. Before very long you learned never to leave a space between yourself and the security of a wall.

The hospital was under the control of a Senior Medical Officer and a Chief Hospital Officer. He had a Hospital P.O. and a team of Hospital Officers, all having received nursing training in addition to basic discipline officer training. No matter in what speciality staff had been trained, they were all prison officers first of all. Decisions relating to medical matters were all down to the S.M.O.

The second detached wing housed non-convicted and civil prisoners, about whom I will go into more detail later.

We toured the reception area, where all prisoners entering or departing the prison were processed following committal by the courts or being taken to court.

Finally, we were shown the prisons workshops, where not much talking was allowed, but as the old saying goes, 'Every picture paints a thousand words.' The looks of contempt or amusement told us their feelings towards new screws. I was instantly recognised as a copper, but strangely enough it didn't cause me any problem what so ever. I think that I was seen as being fair and never trying to stitch anyone up helped me through the initial stages. But, besides this some were planning what sort of a dance they were about to lead us.

Let me say that in all prisons were it not for the goodwill of prisoners, then the system would quickly be doomed to failure.

Discipline and enforcement of regulations were vital ingredients controlling prisoners but so the goodwill of prisoners played an equally essential part.

The tour was completed and we were sent for a very welcomed cuppa, where we renewed acquaintances with some of the staff who we met up with during the first month of training, plus some new faces, all of whom we would be working with in the future.

Teamwork was an essential ingredient in a profession such as ours and much comradeship was built up in the tea rooms and staff clubs. Should an incident occur, then having built up good relationships was half the battle of working together, relying on, and understanding each other was the second half.

Tea break was over, our Supervisors being very hot on time; we re-assembled to receive our welcome/warning from the Governor and the Chief Officer. This didn't take very long, but the text of the address left us in no uncertain terms as to what was expected of us.

First and foremost, we were discouraged from talking to prisoners, unless it was formal to glean information, or give a direct order. Secondly, we were warned about the dangers of trafficking with prisoners, i.e. Fetching or carrying to or from the prison illegal items for reward. If caught this could mean being prosecuted and possibly imprisoned. I was to discover that once you succumbed then pressure was piled on until you could be forced to bring dangerous items in such as a knife or a gun. The demands would always escalate and followed a member of staff wherever he went. There were no hiding places, someone would always know.

The former instruction relating to not talking to prisoners, none of us agreed with because the object to send a prisoner out rehabilitated would have fallen flat on its face.

If conversation was not going to be allowed this would defeat part of building up of a good relationship, because to have a good understanding of each other you must communicate, and no understanding would exist if you couldn't talk with the person concerned. So lets say we modified that order to suit our own purpose, but also for the benefit of the people we were charged with rehabilitating.

First Posting

My colleague and I were allocated to the prisons remand centre, where all non-convicted men who had been remanded in custody for a variety of reasons were located.

Some were held because of the very serious nature of their alleged crimes i.e. Robbery, assault, and sexually motivated crimes. Some, who had been granted bail and were awaiting suitable sureties before being released, others it was feared were liable to interfere with witnesses prior to their trial, or vanish before the court hearing.

These people were, by our law considered to be innocent until proven guilty. By virtue of this they were afforded certain extra privileges convicted prisoners could not have. Examples were; They could wear their own clothes provided they were suitable, obviously they would not be permitted to wear clothes covered in glitter, or conversely rags, but any provided they were within reason. They could spend private cash to purchase extra items, mostly tobacco, but sometimes soap, toothpaste or shampoo was chosen. Other items were allowed for special occasions such as birthday cards or chocolates.

Other less fortunate individuals were not able to buy extras, thus a two-tier system was created, these prisoners could however work if they so chose. Some opted for this but otherwise they had to go without.

I did not see the two-tier system as being a fair way. One so called perk that existed in my earlier days was that a prisoner could – upon payment – have another prisoner to clean his cell. Which to my mind encouraged laziness and made one group servile to another. In these areas of confinement all men should be equal.

The prisons banking system was run by so called barons, tobacco being the main currency. Not many tailor made cigarettes existed, so payments were made in 'roll-ups,' these being hand rolled cigarettes, or quarters, halves or ounces of tobacco. Of course the repayments were at a much higher rate of interest. At this time an ounce of tobacco was rated as equivalent to about £5.

At court, remand prisoners were also allowed to select a barrister to take on their defence, many of which were hopeless tasks. The cost of this was £2.4s 6d, and when the danger of this arose, the more experienced barristers could be seen sliding out of the courtroom, leaving their younger colleagues to take on the task.

Judges having been in this situation in their younger days were alert to this and would ensure that so many remained, so the prisoner was given a choice. One elderly barrister who was blessed with the reputation of winning few cases in his career, would willingly offer his services, and you could hear the prisoners inwardly groan should he be the chosen one. This selection process was known as a 'dock brief.'

Another class of prisoner detained on the remand section was the civil prisoner. They wore brown suits and had to work, they had no extra privileges, and were in for mainly county court debt or contempt of court.

One such prisoner was detained for refusing to disclose his daughter's whereabouts, he stayed in for a long time, until eventually he purged his contempt and informed the powers that be. Another, was a top circus owner, in for debt, but whilst in refused to wash. Many others were in for failure to pay wife maintenance. Call me soft but this group, I felt were exploited.

The danger of detaining people like this is that they tend to become institutionalised, when probably before they had been of good character and had never seen the inside of a prison, were now becoming hardened to the criminal world. They had been educated in how to rob, shoplift or commit fraud. Picking all the tips up via the so-called professional. Why, I've yet to discover. What the answer is I do not know, but certainly, I don't feel it's a prison.

The officer in charge of our unit was of the same grade as we were but had many years' service beneath his belt and that wasn't all that was there, his stomach protruded extensively. I was to learn that he was an ardent beer drinker. Eventually he was moved to another prison on promotion, but his presence still is as clear as ever in my mind. A forbidding character, of whom it took many years to get to know, and then I don't think many people were able to get close to him.

At the establishment at which he ended his days he became known as the Russian P/O. F*** off ski.

After eyeing us up and down he said to me, "See that up there," pointing to the top landing. "Stand in the corner and don't talk to these bastards. Your not getting keys yet because we don't trust sprogs."

The keys he referred to put me in the mind of medieval times, they were huge, perhaps more in line with something used by yeoman warders in the tower.

Prisoners quickly latched on the idea that we were new, and the sob stories came in thick and fast. They were so hard done by, being innocent, and all they wanted was a fair chance to prove their innocence and could we get them a special letter to write and explain the circumstances to their girlfriends. For many this was a crafty way to obtain an extra letter free, they used many other ploys but we soon learned to look for hidden motives.

There weren't any probation officers or welfare staff, so in effect you were expected to act in this capacity, despite talking to prisoners being taboo. It was our job to sift the genuine from the frivolous.

On the day of a court appearance, prisoners tended to be on edge, probably because they knew they could be going to prison, or that they hadn't much chance of being cleared. Either way it was not the ideal time for wise cracks or leg pulls, because you stood a fair chance of wearing a plastic chamber pot, certainly not the fashion of the day!

The officer in charge did not do too much to foster good relations. I remember once his remark to a West Indian lad, "Do you know, I really like you." "Do you boss?" he replied. "Yes, with another nine like you I could get a silver golly badge from Robinson's." Not the most tactful of remarks to make. However, this lad walked away chuckling. I know many that wouldn't have responded so favourably to such a comment.

Another favourite trick of this officer was to drape a tea cloth around his neck and slurp curried beans from a ladle, quite often spilling more beans over his uniform than found their way into his mouth. On this particular day he put too much pressure onto the container with the beans in and upturned it all over his trousers. Totally unperturbed he removed his trousers, wiping them and placed them onto a nearby radiator and carried on serving, attired in long johns and cap. Suddenly the Chief walked in, which would have raised most of us to panic stations. Not him however, he reported his wing as being correct and carried on.

The poor old Chief was totally bewildered shaking his head and thinking, "Why me?" I am sure that he did not know how to cope and its not very often that could be said about a Chief Officer.

Days were fully occupied supervising prisoners' ablutions, meals, exercise, library, work periods and legal visits. Cells were also checked on a routine known as L.B.B. – Locks, bolts and bars – because, although being presumed innocent until found guilty, there were quite a number attempted escapes. We became expert at detecting bars which had been tampered with by their very sound. Many methods to hide tampered bars were used, a favourite being porridge as a substitute for filler. Most of us used a truncheon to test the cell bars, and the number of times that a red faced officer would present the Chief with a truncheon in pieces, meekly asking for a replacement was unbelievable. Of course the Chief was far from being amused and eventually the practice ceased. Anyone, who broke a truncheon from then onwards, paid for it. So as you can imagine not many truncheons were broken.

One entitlement remand prisoners had, was that of one reputed pint of beer or cider, alternatively soft drinks. It was soft drinks that presented the biggest problem, dandelion and burdock smelled remarkably like whiskey, and ice cream soda took on the guise of gin or vodka. Obviously well wishers were trying to warm up the cockles of their hearts, but besides being illegal these cocktails were very dangerous.

It was our responsibility to test these concoctions, so care had to be exercised in case of revenge attacks i.e. Poison or even urine or of obviously becoming intoxicated. Upon looking back, the whole testing method was a dangerous practice, because the mind boggles at what could have been put into the bottles!

On the non-convicted section of prisons, the categories are divided into two. The first one being remand prisoners, who are people remanded into custody pending further appearances before the same level of court. To allow time for further enquires to be made or for the case to be prepared for presentation.

The second category is trials, i.e. Prisoners whose cases have been heard by the lower court and committed to the higher court for trial or sentence.

The criminal courts in this country are divided into two tiers – the lower one being magistrates court, who deal with less serious crimes and have limitations as to what sentences they are able to impose. The higher courts are the crown courts that can impose any sentence up to life imprisonment. A person can elect for a case to be heard by the higher court. The general feeling by the old lags was that they could end up with a better deal from a judge than a magistrate. Although this was not always the case. I have seen a sentence of 10 years imprisonment given out for theft of a bottle of milk in a higher court, whereas they may have received a much lighter sentence in a lower court. So this seems to defeat the argument.

In my earlier days courts were divided into three: Magistrates, Quarter Sessions and Assizes, the latter presided over by top ranking judges, who could pass a death sentence in certain cases, i.e. Murder, Arson, in H M Dockyards piracy and treason.

Quarter Sessions and Assizes were run by the Prison Service and a simple definition of our function was to operate a detached mini jail and to staff the docks in each court.

A Principal Officer would be in charge, and on the day before either a Quarter Session of Assize started he would be in possession of a Court Calendar, giving a list of prisoners due to appear. This process would be repeated on a daily basis.

A few days at court were looked forward to by staff because it took them out of the main prison environment.

The younger staff were expected to do the donkey work, and it was our regular duty prior to departure from the prison, to collect all the food from the kitchen, and collect the prisoners from their various locations.

Most knew what to do and were prepared when we collected them, but the odd few didn't want to go and would make it very difficult. Several times I have been to collect, and found a prisoner barricaded in his cell and hidden under the bed. Getting them out was not an easy task, especially very early in the morning. Some even changed locations, of course they were putting their head on the proverbial chopping block and would face a disciplinary charge upon their return from court. Some of course evaded this by receiving a non-custodial sentence, in which case they didn't return to prison.

The system of taking a prisoner off the roll board was simple if adhered to. There were no short cuts, unfortunately some staff tried to find one, and the end result was of the staff being delayed for up to half and hour for their breakfast. Not the best way to endear good relations.

Each prisoner had a cell card outside their cell – this had to be removed – one deducted from the landing roll, the wing roll and the main prison roll. If this was completed for each prisoner, the physical check should produce the correct numbers, but often it didn't and tempers became frayed.

We haven't even left the prison yet and see the complications which could arise.

All the prisoners were taken to the reception and allowed to change into their own clothes if they were wearing prison uniform. If they wished they were permitted to have a change of clothing brought in for them on a one to one basis.

Their personal property was given to them and they were treated as if being discharged. All were searched and handcuffed in pairs, any odd ones literally or physically were cuffed to an officer, and guess who got that job? Us new ones of course.

If a prisoner presented himself as a threat to security we tried to handcuff him to some one with a disability, or an older person thus reducing the risk of escape. If you could realise that whilst in transit all the security that remained was handcuffs and staff, and on the first day of the court there could be forty prisoners on board, it was a very vulnerable time.

Before departure the coach was checked for weapons or weak links. All keys were handed in and the receipt given was a metal tally with the corresponding number to the keys etched on it. Taking keys out of the prison was regarded as a serious disciplinary offence.

I remember once, the P.O. in charge checking that all staff keys had been handed in, but about halfway to our destination uttered an expletive, because he found that he had still got his own keys. The air became red hot and so did the phone when we arrived. This one was hushed up, but usually the result was that not only the person taking the keys was disciplined, but so was the gate officer for not checking and ensuring this had been done before allowing the coach out of the prison. Sometimes this was easier said than done, with the constant pressure of movement taking place during this peak period.

INSIDE OUT

At Court

As the vehicles arrived at court the area became a hive of activity. The first job was to check that the entire cell area was secure, because it would be no good locating the prisoners in the cells to find that they had quickly hopped it through an insecure window or door. Not only would faces be red, but also there would be much to explain to higher authority, so locking the prisoners up and keeping a roll board was first on the list. After this would be to ensure that those prisoners who wished were allowed to shave, so an officer would be allocated to supervise this activity.

Other officers were allocated to supervise official visits, mostly by defence counsels, sometimes from police or probation service preparing reports for the court. Yet more staff were detailed to receive people surrendering from bail.

Staff also covered the cells. I remember once a cell bell being rung and rung, until the very irate officer attended, ready to give the nuisance a tirade of abuse for constantly ringing the bell. Only to be met by a red, or should I say crimson faced barrister, who had been locked away by mistake. The Barrister far from being amused reported the incident to the senior judge, who I feel saw the lighter side of the incident because nothing was said to our P.O.

As for the officer, he maintained a very low profile, not only for that day but also for several more afterwards.

Below stairs we found most of the Barristers to be great company, many is the time when we have engaged in light hearted conversation, nothing like they appear in court. One particular one was very partial to prison goulash or stew. Many of those I knew are now judges themselves.

Officers were then allocated for dock duty in the various courts. Usually a junior and a senior being paired up. If trouble was expected the number of officers was increased, but usually trouble didn't come until the actual day on which sentence was passed.

Potential flash points were carefully watched for, and it wasn't an unusual event for attacks to be attempted on court officials.

It was for this reason that care had to be exercised when people were received from bail, because amongst other things, they could attempt to secrete weapons on their person, another danger was drugs. Medication was strictly monitored and could not be issued without consent from a trained member of the prison hospital staff, one of which travelled with us to court.

I personally used to search defendants each time they entered or left the dock. I would hate to imagine the repercussions resulting from a judge should he get covered in either ink or flour, or hit by a missile thrown from the dock.

The officer in charge of a dock has a very important role, besides ensuring security; it is his responsibility to ensure that prisoners appear in the correct order. That all the available data and information is at hand, should the court require it. A good dock officer is available to the judge who will often ask for information about the prisoner. He is also responsible for writing down the exact words said by the judge when he passes sentence, because some of the comments may relate to future training and treatment, and indeed the amount of time served.

Some cases are long and tedious; they often last for weeks, particularly company fraud cases, and during one of these cases the officer in charge had dozed off. The prisoner seeing this nudged the officer to waken him. In case the judge noticed, the officer suddenly coming to life for no apparent reason shouts at the top of his voice, "Stand Up," silence reined. The officer was very embarrassed, as for the judge; his look of disgust said it all. The ability to keep awake at times is extremely difficult. However, many people in the court were highly amused. Judges often look to be asleep, but they are not, because should counsel say something probably contrary to what they had previously said; the judge will rapidly pick him up. It is also very evident when the judge sums up he has clearly heard every word.

Dock officers got to recognise different indicators from their charges and to be able to weigh up potential escapers or those likely to cause disruption. Some of the signs, which we used to watch for, were twitching neck muscles and fidgety hands or feet, but much was felt by instinct.

Judges were all powerful and their word was absolute law. I remember on one occasion the P.O. in charge being hauled before the judge, and advised that a smell of onions was permeating the court and as nice as they were to remove the smell post haste or face the consequences. It strangely and slowly disappeared, the P.O. was cautious as to his own safety.

May be some will feel that no man wielded that much power but there was the exception.

Another time, a prisoner due to be produced from a nearby jail had not arrived. The judge enquired from the P.O. as to why. The P.O. explained that the Chief Officer of the jail concerned had a job finding an escort. The judge's reply was "Tell him that I will give him the hour, and unless he wishes to be incarcerated inside his own jail, the prisoner had better be here." He was, and well inside the hour allotted.

It was said, I cannot verify it, that a very senior judge once ordered aeroplanes to be removed out of the sky during an exercise, because they were disrupting proceedings during a big capital murder case. True or not, there weren't many prepared to argue with the might of the law. Sometimes remarks made by judges would cause laughter, during a murder trial; a principal psychologist was giving expert evidence relating to tests carried out on a prisoner. The judge remarked, "What sort of tests?" the expert replied, "What are the warmest and coldest colours?" "What are?" said the judge. "Black is the warmest and white is the coldest". "So," says the judge "How does one account for polar bears?" "They are never cold." This brought peals of laughter.

Other times a judge will lead an illiterate person through the evidence. A particular incident when one such person was being led during a rape case, phases such as, "Did she get it out," and "Did you come your cocoa" were used.

Of course, whatever was said we had to keep a straight face, despite the fact that our stomachs ached with the want for bursting out laughing.

Another judge used to pass tips when his racehorses were running. Many are the time he has given us a winner.

Despite being shrewd and having a lot of power. I found them to be very human and often possessing a wicked sense of humour.

The court P.O. in the prison often was in charge of the wing holding some of the prisoners up for trial or sentence, and this had a remarkably calming effect for even the worst troublemaker, for fear that the judge may ask a verbal report when passing sentence.

I think that plea bargaining was used even during my service, especially when a guilty plea could save an awful lot of time and excessive expense, and the chances were that the defendant would receive a somewhat lighter sentence than he would have got, had he pleaded not guilty!

Tall stories offered in defence would quickly be shot down by a few well-chosen words uttered by the judge.

As the day progressed and prisoners were sentenced, so the reception area of the court sprung to life. The same procedure would take place as in the prison, starting with searching and listing of prisoner's property. Once, on these reception searches we found secreted on the man's person enough cigarettes to start a tobacconists. He wore a gabardine raincoat and most carefully cello-taped were rows of cigarettes. His intention was not only to use for himself, but also to sell at a profit to others. Anyway, he failed in his attempt; because convicted men are restricted to the amount of tobacco they may have.

Itemising property was important and entering exactly what the item was saved much trouble later. To say a pen, was not good enough, because come discharge day a pen would always become a Parker or similar. Likewise, a cheap watch would become an Omega, whereas a little attention to detail would save a lot of aggravation later.

If the entry made were, 'cheap plastic disposable pen' then no one would be left in any doubt as to its real value. If the opportunity arose, a prisoner would attempt to exploit the situation.

The idea of completing the reception records at court was to save time for staff working at the prison's reception. When arriving back at the main prison, which was quite often late at night, also a number of courts within the catchment area would be running at the same time. The last thing staff would wish for late at night, would be an influx of prisoners to be put through the reception routine and located.

At the completion of the day's business, the clerk of the court would provide a list of defendants required for the following day, plus any witnesses who were in custody. These lists would give an indication as to how many staff was required.

It was the P.O. in charges responsibility to ensure that the prisons administration staff were aware of the following days requirements and the necessary arrangements were made for the prisoners to be available for court. Some of which were detained in other prisons, so staff at those prisons was required to ensure these people, either defendants or witnesses attended on time.

From the list, often the P.O. would know his required manning levels. He would look for potentially known troublemakers or escape risks.

I have known seven officers for one man, or conversely one officer for seven prisoners. If the case was a company fraud and the people in the dock were all company directors, the case would possibly last for weeks and limited supervision would be required. It would be unlikely that trouble would erupt.

Most of the troublemakers would be well known to us, often from previous court appearances, so the necessary arrangements would be made.

Court reception officers would be preparing records for convicted prisoners, other officers supervising official visits.

Some visits were carried out 'in sight' but 'out of hearing' of the officer, and amongst these were visits from legal advisors.

Another officer would be responsible for serving the tea meal and cleaning up. Often young offenders would be pleased to help out and sometimes it gave them chance for extra food or perhaps a cigarette.

On occasions, a young prisoner would be sentenced to detention, this meant that they would have to be collected from the court direct by Detention Centre Staff, or we would have to escort them, because under no circumstances were they allowed back into prison.

From Birmingham we had three detention centres available. Two local, but one in Devises, Wiltshire. After a full day at court this was very tiring. Often we would arrive back during the small hours, and still required to report for duty at 0700 hours, very sleepy and not in a very good frame of mind.

Those remaining worked together and it was quite a good thing to allow a domestic visit, either with loved ones or parents. This helped on many occasions to diffuse the situation or calm an angry person. Also, it gave the prisoner a chance to hand out property, quite often a large amount. This would assist us because storage space was limited in the prison's reception.

The coach would then arrive; again the same check would take place, a search of the coach and then escorting the prisoners, two at a time into the vehicle.

Despite being tired, staff had to be very alert because the security link was very weak from then onwards until they reached their destination. Bearing in mind that some had just received fairly lengthy sentences, and this was their last chance to make a dash for freedom.

Once a Warwick Assize, as two prisoners were being walked back to the coach, they broke free from their escort and ran towards Warwick, still handcuffed together. Staff gave chase. The two escapees were making good headway but unfortunately for them, they ran either side of a lamppost, the handcuffs acting as a pivot brought on a collision of heads. Staff had by then arrived and there was no problem apprehending two semi-conscious men.

Apart from sore heads they had a lot of living down to do from their fellow prisoners the following morning. Comments such as, "Getting a head start," or "Not making a good headway" certainly did not go down too well.

Should a prisoner become extremely violent or disruptive, then it was always good policy to arrange for a taxi and escort them back to prison separately. Going back with a coach load of prisoners, probably some of who had just been sentenced could prove to be a delicate situation, especially with a disruptive prisoner on board.

I have to say that despite what faced them, the majority of prisoners were well behaved during these journeys.

Court Security

Some of the cells at courts were, and in fact, in certain places still are badly sited. For example, at one court the cell windows looked onto a footpath and contraband was being passed in to newly convicted prisoners. Unfortunately for them, in an empty cell next to theirs an officer using the cell toilet overheard a conversation from relatives to the men in the cell, and after the items had been handed in we quickly retrieved them. The items, particularly tobacco would have been rapidly shared out amongst other inmates to carry back into prison, and then collected back afterwards, this would ensure that no one would be carrying any more than their legal entitlement when searched.

At another court, as a prisoner was being taken from the dock after sentence the escort had to pass a coalhole, which was insecure. The prisoner as quick as a flash jumped his escort, ran into the area and out through the coal chute. Unfortunately, he had covered himself in coal dust, which made it relatively easy for his quick apprehension.

There are many horror stories I could relate about insecure courts. I'll conclude by telling you of one that had no cells what so ever. The prisoner and his escort sat on a bench in a room, which was used communally by the public and was totally insecure. The strange fact was that we never lost a prisoner from here. Possibly it was because we were aware of the problem and on our guard all the while, or just good luck. Who knows?

In my opinion in the early days many courts were designed without much thought being given towards security what so ever, except from the physical aspect. The criticism should have been directed equally toward the design, rather than lay all the blame on the officer, which would happen if an escape took place.

Other vulnerable areas were courtrooms, many of which had very insecure docks, for example, low rails that could easily be jumped. Some courts had several doors; each leading to freedom via the outside halls of courts, especially if police officers manning the doors had been temporarily distracted.

Another tense time was when prisoners were being taken from the docks to the witness boxes or being returned.

In some courts, prisoners who were required in a certain court may have to be taken to the appropriate one via the public halls, many of which were literally a 'stones throw' from the busy streets and freedom, presenting a serious threat to security.

Escorts

Apart from court duties the prison officer has other responsibilities outside the confines of the prison.

Which are, carrying out escort duties for a variety of reasons, for example, transfer of prisoners to other establishments, producing prisoners at the lower courts, to hospitals for treatment or visiting very sick relatives under going hospitalization. Attending funerals of close relatives.

Escorting prisoners is a very vulnerable time for staff, because once you have driven outside the prison gates you become a mini prison on wheels. Gone is the high perimeter wall, and the secure cell, numbers of staff are dramatically reduced and this is where temptation becomes greater, especially if the person is tensed up.

It is for the staff to interpret the situation from intelligence information, or simply gut feelings, because they are wholly responsible from departure to return or arrival at their destination.

Sometimes, information is received via inmates. One day I was about to take an escort to a City nearby for simple remand procedures. Whilst in reception, a prisoner who was normally quiet and pro staff began abusing and threatening me. I had no option but to lock him in his cell. As I was doing this – which incidentally was what he wanted me to do – He said, "There's going to be an escape. It's the one you are taking and the gangs are going to be tooled up (armed)."

I immediately reported this to my superiors and the escort strength was tripled, also it was re-inforced by several police vehicles. The man we were taking was facing charges of armed robbery.

As we left the prison a look out man was given the thumbs down signal by the prisoner, so we presumed he was in contact with the gang. There were no gang, only road cones and signs where we presumed was the spot intended to spring him.

Upon arrival at the court the faces of his waiting cronies was a sight to behold.

We were informed that the gang was going to pretend to be a road gang with the usual stop/go sign. They would cone off part of the road, use the stop signal, and whilst stationary they intended to free the prisoner. We rely a great deal on receiving this type of information, even more so on this occasion, which if events turned out as planned could have been very nasty.

Escorts to hospitals are also extremely vulnerable, because of certain rulings relating to releasing prisoners from restraints. The rule was; the cuffs were taken off as they entered the treatment room, but some hospital staff required them to be released long before this because of upsetting other patients, causing disagreements between prison and hospital staff.

Many escapes have taken place from hospitals and clinics, but one outstanding one I recall was from a limb fitting centre, happening whilst his wooden leg was being adjusted.

Emblazoned across the local paper were the words, "One legged man hops it."

The other prisoners saw the man as something of a hero, but the escorting staff became the butt of many humorous comments, such as, "Can you do my escort, promise I won't hop off."

Whilst on the subject of wooden legs, one prisoner patient used to have to visit a limb fitting centre, and the number of stolen items he stacked into his artificial leg was unbelievable. He had combs, razors, mugs, cutlery, etc. The objective was to exchange these for tobacco with other outpatients and smuggle it back and sell it in the prison. However, the hospital officer who used to take him was wise to his tricks, and the last thing he did before the escorts departure was to shake all the contents out.

Funeral escorts were times when extreme discretion was needed. I for one did not like to encroach too far into another's grief, but it was also a time when ill feelings could come out and if you were not careful you could finish up involved in a family feud.

Escorts of top security prisoners involved police patrol cars that would take us through their respective areas at break neck speeds, much to the great delight of the top security prisoner. I think that the sooner that they got through their areas the better for us, as we were saddled with the prisoner, usually a high risk one until we arrived at our destination.

Although I inwardly breathed a sigh of relief each time we arrived safely at our destination, I must say that I enjoyed this duty as much if not more than any other did.

Maybe, due to the fact that throughout my service I never lost a prisoner, I think my secret was to engage them in conversation and keep their minds fully occupied, because whilst they were talking they were not thinking of more devious things. Of course you also had to be constantly vigilant.

To highlight this an escort, which set off for a court production, resulted in the prisoner escaping after very badly injuring two prison officers, one of whom never returned to work. Not only did the prisoner carry out these assaults, but he also murdered an entire family in their cottage, this horrific chapter closed when the man was shot dead by police marksman.

This is why staff must remain totally on the alert, because it happens when it is least expected. Something, which started as a relatively straightforward routine escort, ended up as a horror story. No prisoner should be underestimated when considering risk assessment.

As a very junior officer, I was once detailed to report to reception where a very senior officer met me with a beaming smile.

I was soon to discover why? The prisoner we were escorting was called. "Stick your hand out Richard" the officer said. Looking, I could not believe what I had seen, because the prisoner was in full female attire. The officer looked, remarking "You make an ideal couple." I wasn't amused feeling somewhat embarrassed. However I consoled myself with the fact that it was much better than being handcuffed to some old tramp that needed fumigating.

The person in question was undergoing a sex change, and later, after the operation decided to end his own life.

During this period private hire cars were contracted and during one escort I instructed the driver to stop and request a replacement taxi. He was not fit to drive, not because of drink or drugs but because of his inability to drive safely.

Escorts as you can see are extremely important and responsible duties. Not only are you responsible for the security and safety of the prisoner and the public, but also ensuring that all the correct documentation is there, especially when handing over to police or court authorities and that the prisoner has all his entitled cash and property.

JUST ROUTINE

A Fixed Post At Last

As I was beginning to accrue some service I became eligible to have a 'Fixed Post.' This meant that for a twelve-month period I would carryout one specific job of which, there were some very interesting ones, such as a prisoner reception, gate-chief, officer's clerk or canteen officer.

As I entered the Chief's office I was planning which job I would get, maybe if it wasn't one of those, it would be the block or censor, one that I had forgotten was the dreaded one – The bath house, and guess the job I was given? Yes, the bathhouse, seen by staff as the rottenest job of all. Stuck amongst stinking socks and gungy undies, however, I didn't get any choice – It was, the you will! Not, will you.

Two of us operated this post, which was to ensure that every prisoner received a full change of clothing weekly.

Normally parties were collected from their places of work in-groups of twenty, one of us had to walk and collect the party until the workshop was completed. Whilst collection or return of prisoners was in progress, the situation could be very risky, because during my time on this job staff were not issued with radios, in fact, they were not in use until the late sixties. If a prisoner decided to try to escape or disrupt a party then you would have to pray or shout very loud to gain assistance.

As the prisoners changed their clothing they were issued with the clean items, neatly rolled up during this interchange, care had to be taken because of items being hidden amongst the bundles. Items such as tobacco, money or weapons were some things, which would have to be watched for. The main item, which was likely to be contained amongst the dirty linen, was letters or messages intended for outside.

The clothing exchange store was adjacent to the bathhouse and run by civilian storeman, it presented an ideal go between for inside and outside of the prison. Most stores staff were completely trust worthy, but in our line of business you could never be too careful and working amongst prisoners could make some types gullible, especially if pressure was applied. Say for example, threats against family or even the person concerned being threatened with violence when outside of the prison and off duty. It wasn't uncommon for 'ex-cons' and staff to use the same pubs.

At that time censorship of mail was strictly enforced so smuggling out letters via this method would be the ideal way to by-pass authority.

The bath water was not permitted to exceed a certain depth and our first Governor walked with a walking stick, which had a carefully cut out notch at the exact depth at which the water should be. He would insert this into baths at random, and woe betide staff if the water was over the statutory depth. It didn't matter if it was under, but if it was over, the officer could watch out.

The heating system was always suspect and the water was always running cool, many people still had baths in it after receiving some first class sales-manship from staff, who convinced them that the water was not really cold – just that the temperature had dropped. I know one thing for certain; I wouldn't have relished reclining for long in such water.

Some didn't want to bath at all. Others didn't want to get out and some bathed in a very strange way! For example, my orderly called me one day and pointed out one such character laying in the bath, fully clothed – even with his boots and socks on and NO water whatsoever in the bath.

The orderly who was responsible for the collection and return of clothing to each stable type bathroom was constantly involved in arguments; clothing without buttons, torn clothing or socks with holes in, but apart from being very physically fit he was also diplomatic – I think!

If a prisoner was a security risk he was bathed separately to enable us to maintain better supervision, and it was during one of these supervised sessions that we received information that the man was planning to escape and he was possibly armed. Other staff were brought in and tactfully every item he possessed was thoroughly searched. Fortunately, nothing happened and nothing was found, but it was a very tense half-hour. The man was a very high-risk prisoner and did eventually escape, but not from our prison thank goodness.

Like every job, it is what you make of it and we had adapted the system to work ideally, it was with some reluctance that I moved on, because in a strange way I started to enjoy it, but someone else would be moving in and no doubt I would be returning to plodding the landing and acquainting myself with their associated smells. UGH!

But how wrong I was.

Another fixed post

As the change over date approached, fully expecting a return to pounding the landings I was summoned to the Chief's office and told that I would be taking over the duties of canteen officer.

A totally new concept of prisoner control to me.

Each prisoner was paid a wage of three shillings and fivepence unless his wage had been restricted by a stoppage of his earnings. This could be imposed by the internal disciplinary system.

Three and fivepence allowed the prisoner to purchase half an ounce of hand rolling tobacco, a packet of cigarette papers and a box of safety matches – red matches were not allowed.

Prisoners were expert in splitting matches into four and the cigarettes were not much thicker than a match this ration had to be eked out to last a full week.

Some prisoners would earn more being employed on special jobs.

The ward canteen conjures up an image of catering but this is not so in prison – it means an outlet where they are able to spend their wages.

In the majority of prisons no cash exchanged hands – it was merely a paper transaction – the amount spent being entered and the balance carried over to credit. The prisoner would then sign to say he agreed.

The nature of prisoners being as it is and seeing new faces some would attempt manipulated staff. One of the favourite tricks would be to queue up collect their goods and fail to sign returning later innocently as though this was their first visit or to come back appearing flustered saying "I've forgotten my *snout Gov" ie trying to obtain a second issue of tobacco. Another would be to swear blind that someone else had signed in their place on the pay sheet and they had not in fact received the items.

Sometimes they had to be physically ejected to show that you meant business should you fall for it then those trying you on would increase and the problem became a nightmare.

Weekly on a Monday an outside supplier would deliver the stock ordered but the unloading was a big problem. It was a long walk from the nearest drop off point to the canteen – We carried the tobacco – but other items were in equal demand a favourite being sugar which wasn't just used to sweeten but also to assist in the manufacture of illicit alcohol brews. The journey was along a corridor up a flight of spiral stairs to the canteen. Occasionally items would disappear on the journey to the canteen – this being rapidly 'split up' never to be seen again, so constant vigilance was essential.

If some item vanished then it was very rare that a loss was shown because a penny here and there soon made up the deficit when catering for nearly a thousand people.

Prisoners were permitted to place special orders for goods not sold by us – within certain limitations e.g. birthday cards, Christmas cards, different tobacco brands, soaps and toothpaste – the latter. I can't blame them because the issue toothpowder tasted just like powdered chalk – I know because I've tried it.

One day whilst working away in the canteen we heard a tremendous roar and a commotion coming from the floor below – we looked out and saw the reason – whilst fighting one prisoner had jumped on another's back and bitten his ear off. The ear quickly taken to hospital where an attempt was made to re-stitch it on, but without success. Modern microsurgery may have produced a better result.

Officially we were not permitted to start serving until the evening but often we were able to sneak small groups in during the day – I might add at our peril should the Chief catch us.

When capital punishment was abolished the condemned cell was converted into a purpose built canteen – ideal – large counters with plenty of display space and enough room to carry out work on the pay sheets unlike the little pokey hole we had before.

Occasionally when everything had been balanced and the stock replenished we would have the odd game of crib and this time whilst my opponent was deliberating, we sat in silence when three sharp knocks came from the door of the old execution chamber. I said to my colleague 'Pack up messing around' he denied being responsible. We both placed our arms and hands on the table and again three knocks. If it was a practical joke I do not know how the perpetrator gained entry. From then onwards I was extremely cautious when entering the room especially on my own. Probably a clever practical joke but I didn't hang around to find out.

Twice weekly unconvicted prisoners were allowed to purchase items from their own private cash so twice a week we would have to take a basket of items to the remand wing and deal with their requests. This is the 'two-tier' system I refer to before because the less fortunate without private means could have nothing extra except for a small amount of earnings if they elected to work.

I had two enjoyable years and learnt much about people which helped towards the future, especially my new post because, once again escaping the rigours of landing duties I was to find myself confronted with probably one of the most challenging posts in my career as punishment block officer where I would meet some of the most devious and dangerous men imaginable.

The Chokey Block

This is the every day expression used by staff and inmates alike, when referring to the segregation unit of a prison.

Chokey was originally a diet of bread and water, awarded as a punishment. Hence the term 'Chokey Block,' because in the old days this would be the usual sentence meted out by the prison Governors.

Every prison houses its anti-social type prisoners who in their opposition to authority and its rules have to be disciplined, otherwise, if they are seen as getting away with breaches, others would follow suit and before long the entire prison would be in turmoil.

To deal with this section of prison, rules were devoted to providing cover by which prison officers were able to place offenders on a Governors report.

The block was the place where the offenders were detained pending adjudication - Adjudicated on and finally located to serve any punishment which involved any restriction to normal prison routines, for example, confined to cell or removed from associated labour.

Mainly its occupants were anti-authority or anti-social and many times both.

Most prisoners would serve their sentence and avoid a visit to the block throughout the entire period they were our guests, some however, fell foul for minor breaches, they would accept the punishment awarded, serve it and get back to the main prison.

This type however caused little trouble and were accepted by most staff, on the other hand the anti-authoritarian was totally resistant to rules and could quite often be a danger to staff. It was for this reason that only one man was unlocked at a time.

There is an old saying in prison which goes like this, "If you can't do the time, then don't commit the crime." Very appropriate to this type of individual.

It was always a good policy never to turn your back on these characters, because if an attack was going to happen, then it would be from the rear more often than not. As you unlocked a cell door you would only partially open it, leaving the prisoner to open the rest. Obviously, if any attack was being planned and you opened the cell door fully, then you presented a very open target.

The most common forms of assault were by throwing the contents of a chamber pot, or a direct assault quite often by the occupant kicking the door - which opened inwards - back at you. We would also 'spring the lock,' meaning pressing a catch which would operate the bolt, stopping it being locked on you whilst you were inside the cell - Once in the prisoner has a perfect hostage.

A prisoner, notorious for throwing the contents of chamber pots at staff, had been sent from another prison to us, for what is known as a 'cooling off period,' - which meant, he was transferred to calm down and then would be returned to his parent prison or to a different one, depending on the circumstances. When he arrived, he was located in a cell in which was a chamber pot half full of liquid covered by a lid. We told him that if he was going to do it, then now was the time. He stared at us, walked past to the 'slop out,' sink tipped the contents out - which incidentally was only water - rinsed it and returned to his cell saying, "Nice one boss - you won't have any trouble from me." He was true to his word.

Maybe this would be seen as provocation, but I know one thing, it worked.

I found that in all areas of a prison, especially the block, if you showed any sign of apprehension or fear, the opportunist would take every advantage to exploit it, often using you as the scapegoat. If a question was asked - say something which a prisoner was not entitled -and the answer was to be 'No,' then it was favourite to say just that! Making no compromise whatsoever, because a compromise to a prisoner was as good as saying 'Yes' and that is when life becomes a nightmare. He would either pester the life out of you until you said yes, or if you said no, an explosive situation could easily erupt.

First thing after breakfast we were responsible for collecting and locating any prisoners, who had been placed on report for acts of indiscipline. This was a time that called for caution because tension would probably be running high.

Each day brought something different, you didn't know what you would face as you unlocked the cell doors on the block. Individual prisoners had to be quickly assessed, carefully judging mood swings, especially those new occupants, remembering that most individuals were located by way of a control problem.

It may have been the result of a fight, where special care had to be taken, because if for example, the two fighters cells were unlocked together, you could be faced with an entire repeat performance and a lot of explaining to do.

It maybe one man who had assaulted staff and he would have to be watched, for fear he assaulted you or it could be someone located pending an investigation, again care had to be taken as to how he was spoken to and what was spoken about. Discretion was certainly called for.

Most prisoners dined in their cells and after collecting their meals on a steel compartment tray - a lethal weapon in itself. Many of them would pass through the block returning to their cells with a tray in one hand and a mug of tea in the other, we had to try, try being the operative word, to ensure that nothing was spilt. The block was a show piece, the floor polished throughout the day with black polish and carefully buffed up with a bumper. The dustbin galvanised and gleaming. It was the block cleaner's pride and joy and he was our secret weapon to ensure that the smallest amount possible was spilt.

The majority of prisoners were careful, but again a small minority couldn't care less, or deliberately spilt the contents, particularly young prisoners. The cleaner, Bill was a frail old man, but he scared the living daylights out of youngsters by his ferocious yelling - us too, I might add, but I must say it had the desired effect. He wasn't over popular with other inmates, so much so, that one day one of them offered him a sandwich, which he gratefully received until he found out its contents - Human excreta - The small minds of some people and the lengths they will go to, in order to carry out their evil deeds is beyond belief.

Still whilst there remains people willing to carry out acts such as this, there will always be the need for people to supervise them.

My term on the block was coming to a close. I had enjoyed the challenge, but working in an isolated environment becomes, after a time, very wearing. I was looking forward to moving out into the wider expanse and meeting more people, but not for long, because I was appointed as part of a team to organise the setting up of a control room within the prison. I was fast becoming known as being, 'excused prisoners,' despite the fact that I had been handling some of the dregs of humanity for the past two years.

Although the block was a place where we were constantly alert, the working comradeship was excellent.

Probably, this was one of the most rewarding posts of my entire service; I gained much experience in handling difficult and dangerous situations and to be able to make on the spot decisions.

We have met with many different forms of resistance, from direct violence by assault attempts, to barricading of cell doors to stop us from entering - even to hiding under a bed and this is probably one of the hardest tasks, because of space being so limited. It was also safest policy to carryout a thorough search on the prisoner, to ensure that no weapons had been hidden upon him. Weapons found, have been home made knives, knuckle dusters, sharpened hacksaws, blades, glass and a whole host of other items. None of which would enhance the complexion.

Sometimes a prisoner would use himself as the protest. On two occasions, prisoners had confronted us smeared with excreta - the lowest of the low - Not a pleasant job cleaning them up.

Once, when females were occupying part of the prison, a woman smeared her entire body with grease - each day she had saved her margarine for such an occasion - plastering it over her. Gripping was an impossibility. She also packed a strong right hook, being the sister of a very famous champion boxer.

Sometimes, disciplinary awards entailed moving beds and bedding from the cell and when I joined the service you could easily identify the prisoners serving punishment, because the beds could be seen scattered on the landings of the entire prison. At suppertime they were allowed to have their beds back in. It was our job to supervise this manoeuvre. One particular day, this tired middle-aged prisoner emerged and commenced lifting his bed to return it to his cell, he seemed to have a struggle, so my colleague attempted to help him out of his predicament by assisting. He firmly put the frame on the floor and informed my colleague, that he had been given the punishment, so not to help him saying, "Guv, I've been given Chokey - not you - so leave it alone." Strange what some see as principals.

The Chief Officer's clerk would bring the day's reports, the prisoners' records to us and we would sort the reports into what we thought was a sensible sequence. Why? I don't know, because each Governor, without exception changed the order around.

We would then await the Governors arrival. I remember on this particular occasion, the Wing Principal officer visited the block to have a quick smoke - he hand rolled his cigarettes and the tobacco he used was obnoxious, it was a cheap product sold to prisoners - He lit-up, taking a deep draw covering us in foul smelling smoke, then posing the question, "Officer, what time does the Governor arrive?" I duly advised him that if he cared to look on the landing above, then he would see the Governor escorted by the Chief approaching. Quick as a flash, he nipped his cigarette out, bringing himself to attention; he saluted the Governor and said to me, "If I catch you smoking again I'll put you on a charge." I was lost for words, but I am certain that the Governor was fully aware who the culprit really was. Despite the fact that he has passed away, I have never forgiven him for pulling such a crafty trick and watch every corner in case he decides to haunt me.

Adjudication's had their lighter moments as well as tensions. On one occasion a prisoner appearing before the Governor was wearing a hearing aid. As the adjudicator started to read out the charge, he was interrupted by the prisoner, pausing to adjust his hearing aid. The Governor continued only to be stopped again, another adjustment made and told to continue.

So this is how the adjudication went throughout, with the Governor and the Chief carefully mouthing the words and using their own versions of sign language. Eventually this farce was completed. The offence was only minor and it didn't warrant us keeping him on the block. I returned him to his location but he could not stop laughing. I asked him what the joke was, but he refused to tell me. I discovered the answer the following day from another prisoner - the hearing aid was completely useless, it had no batteries in and better than that, the prisoner was not even deaf - He had borrowed it from his mate just to play a practical joke on the Governor.

A marvellous actor, who if the Governor had discovered was playing a prank, would probably have been an ex-living human being!

Working on a block dealing with volatile characters day in and day out required teamwork. If you consider that in dealing with every eventuality, it was essential that you and your colleagues were united. You needed someone who you could trust and in turn could trust you. As time progressed you became able to anticipate one anothers actions.

I had throughout, worked with excellent colleagues and thankfully nothing went drastically wrong. This is not to say that everyday was a 'bed of roses,' far from it, but simply, when pressures arose you were all working in the same direction.

Governors, also realising that to have a block running smoothly and efficiently played a large part in how the prison ran overall and as time passed, tended to become less formal with the block staff. We used to have many an interesting chat on a wide variety of subjects, ranging from sport to politics.

Some of their comments during adjudications were priceless. During one hearing, the prisoner was vehemently denying his alleged offence, saying that the officer was lying. The Governor banged his pen on the desk, looked up at the prisoner and said, "My officers do not lie! If they said to me you were riding a motorbike around the top landing in the prison, I would want to know where you had got the petrol from."

If an offence is seen as too serious for the Governor to deal with, he will hear the evidence and refer it to be heard by the Board of Visitors, who were empowered to award higher penalties than the prison Governor.

This could happen to a repetitive offender or in the case of offences where, statute provided no alternative but to refer a case to a Board of

Visitors - An example would be a serious assault by a prisoner on staff or another inmate or an escape from prison.

It is a statutory requirement for both the Governor and the Medical Officer to visit anyone undergoing punishment or cellular confinement on a daily basis.

Not usually on the first day however, especially if the visiting Governor was the one who had awarded the punishment. This would be like putting a red rag to a bull and quite a number are upset at this stage. As the day wears many seem to mellow and become calmer. I will not say this for all, because some will continue to protest throughout the stay.

I personally felt that it was a question of approach. Handled in the correct manner the smouldering fuse could be slowly put out. Conversely, handled incorrectly and you would be faced with an explosion. If a man had been awarded a specific punishment, then I tended to let him get on with it rather than agitate the situation.

Whilst on the subject of approach, it was told that years ago a complaining prisoner was visited by a priest, who sympathetically listened to the prisoners complaints and then proceeded to box his ears. Of course, when the prisoner was visited by the Governor, he told him that the priest had struck him, he was disbelieved and the complaint dismissed. I wouldn't have believed him either, although we did have a visiting monk, who besides being very popular with the younger prisoners ruled them with his own form of discipline.

To conclude this story it was said that following the incident, the priest returned to his chapel, removed his clerical order and re-attired himself in his prison officer's uniform and continued with his duties. The prisoner saw the protest as being hopeless and gave up the ghost. When eventually he returned to normal location he visited the priest who did not identify in any way as the person who had visited him on the block.

The Adjudication

In a prison maintaining standards is essential. Many are basic. All are in the interest of keeping good order and discipline which if allowed to get out of hand could lead to nasty situations, even riots. Prisoners to some extent flock together and they tend to follow the leader. The basic rules of group culture show this and therefore it is vital that a prison governor leads from the front. To assist him there are within prison rules a code of offences ranging from minor to major breaches, for example, being in possession of extra issued articles, to being in possession of an offensive weapon. Using insolent abusive or other improper language to using gross personal violence to an officer.

The Governor, who, in his own right was equivalent to a magistrate, dealt with each offence at the first stage, his powers were limited, but if the offence warranted it, he could refer it to the higher authority. Even to an outside court and in some cases this was the only option. However, the majority of cases were comparatively minor and were dealt with through the internal system.

For the purpose of this example, we will imagine that two officers are conducting a routine cell search in a medium security prison. One officer is in the cell and one outside with the prisoner. Whilst checking the underneath of a cell table, the officer discovers a £10 Bank of England note neatly wedged into the crack. The prisoner is asked for an explanation as to why the note is there, bearing in mind that no money is allowed in this prison. He admits the offence saying, "Fair cop Guv."

The officer making the find would report the facts to his Superior and hand the bank note over with his report. The other officer would be named as a witness. The Superior officer would consider the facts and ask himself if there was a charge under prison rules to cover this offence. He would discover that the offence would be covered by, "Has in his cell room or possession any unauthorised article," namely one £10 Bank of England note.

On the following morning, the prisoner would be relocated under segregation and would be served with a notice of report – commonly known as a telegram by prisoners. Two officers must serve this at least two hours before hand, giving him the opportunity to prepare his defence and call any witnesses. A notice of report lays out the charge in simple terms and includes the name of the reporting officer. The prisoner is allowed to write his explanation on the reverse. If he is not able to write, an officer will be detailed to help him.

The Medical Officer must see the prisoner. This traditionally was to determine his fitness, or otherwise to undergo certain types of punishment. A favourite when I was a young officer being bread and water. Unlikely for this type of offence, but some Governors had strange ideas.

All the documentation, charge sheet, evidence and the confiscated note would be placed in the adjudication room. The Governor would arrive at around 10.30am escorted by the Chief Officer. The prisoner would be escorted to the room where the case was being heard. In my days on the block the prisoner faced the Governor standing about four feet away. The two-man escort faced the prisoner with hands crossed, protecting a vital piece of their anatomy. I would not like to count the number of times that violence has erupted in the adjudication room and woe betide any officers if the Governor gets attacked. Also, it's very uncomfortable if an officer gets kicked, 'you know where'. Nowadays the prisoner and escort are seated – the reason being, it is much easier to restrain a man in a sitting position and it is much harder for him to become violent whilst seated.

Our prisoner would have been searched as he entered the adjudication room. He would be identified and asked if he had been given enough time to prepare his defence and that the notice of report had been served. These facts once established, the charge would be read to the prisoner. He would be asked to plead – guilty or not and if he understood the charge. The officer reporting is called and he gives evidence. In our case it should be fairly straightforward. The prisoner would be given a chance to ask the officer questions.

All would be written by the Governor in long hand. This is very time consuming, especially in a complicated case where a prisoner pleads not guilty and calls half a dozen witnesses. The prisoner would be asked for his version of events. A decision would be reached and a punishment given. More than likely he would receive either a fine or loss of privileges. The money would also be confiscated.

The Chief Officer would ensure the prisoner's record was endorsed with the award given and that the punishment had been carried out.

All documents would then be sent to the Prison Department Legal Branch for vetting. The Governor, for this reason must be very careful, because I have seen cases thrown out simply because of wrong wording. Even more so I would imagine in this day and age of litigation.

Block Team

Another responsibility whilst a member of the 'Block' team, was to act as relief for officers meal breaks who were on duty in the condemned cell.

Let me explain. Should a prisoner receive a sentence of death, then the following routine came into operation. The prisoner would be immediately returned from the court to a special type of accommodation, which was completely self-contained.

All officers, on what was known as 'C C' Duty, would be waiting at their own establishments for the call. No officer would come from the prison responsible for carrying out the sentence until the day the sentence was to be carried out. Then the officers who had been with the prisoner since the day he received his sentence would return to their own establishments and be replaced by two specialist officers from the prison where the execution would take place. They would see the entire routine carried out and then go off duty.

Our job was to relieve the officers on detached duty for their meal breaks and over two or three months you came to know the person very well. In fact, of those who wished to talk probably were more revealing to us than even their own mothers. They seemed, with very few exceptions to accept the inevitable.

When I was assigned to this duty it was the period when the abolition of capital punishment was taking place and of the seven I sat with – not one received this ultimate fate.

This however, did not stop the entire ritual taking place – should a person in the condemned cell have to be moved to the visits room to see either his lawyers or family and friends, or go out for statutory exercise, then the entire prison would have to be locked away – no other prisoner would be allowed to see the condemned man.

The murders they had been convicted of ranged from domestic to murder of a police officer, plus murder whilst committing a robbery or a burglary.

As I say, the formalities had to be carried out, including shaving them with a safety razor, supervising visits to the toilet and bath – a log was also maintained. Prisoners also wore very special clothing, which could cause them no harm should they decided to try to take their own life. Food was also carefully checked.

During the time we held such prisoners, you could detect a change in the mood of the other prisoners and tension would build according to the type of murder. If it was a child murderer, such comments as, "Not long now you bastard," could be heard from outside as the prisoners passed by to and from work – but if they had sympathy for other types of murderer, then comments would be directed towards authority.

One day whilst performing this duty I was unwell and remember being revived by my colleague and the prisoner under sentence of death. Not too many can make that claim to fame. This man was not executed – his sentence being commuted to life imprisonment, however not too long after he met his maker, suffering a massive heart attack. Poetic Justice? Maybe!

Part of our job was to occupy the person and some enjoyed cards or dominoes. I have a story to tell about both, but cards first.

This man had broken out from a low security prison and murdered a scrap dealer who he claimed had cheated him. I don't know about his past credentials, but as for cards I have never met a bigger cheat.

The second story is about the domino player who was also under sentence of death. At a certain stage of the game he seemed to be deep in his own thoughts. "Come on" I said, "Your drop," without thinking about what I had said – "Not yet Mr P." Talk about straight words and crooked thinking – Not the most tactful words to direct towards a man due to hang!

The period between sentence and the day of execution was very busy. Inevitably every prisoner so sentenced would lodge an appeal and the days would be taken up by counsels' visits and medical boards until every avenue had been exhausted. The stay of execution was often granted in the last week – It could be that fresh evidence had come to light or technicalities had arisen relating to the manner in which the trial had been conducted or a point of law. Whatever the reason it had to be thoroughly investigated to give the condemned man every opportunity.

If all failed, then preparations were made for the sentence to be carried out.

The Governor would be responsible for keeping the prisoner updated with the stages of the appeal and of the final decision.

The prisoner would be visited by the Prison Chaplain and the Medical Officer daily.

The person responsible for carrying the sentence out would also make preparations. Shortly before the due day, we would view the prisoner as he was taken out to exercise and estimate the physical details of the prisoner i.e. height and weight. The mechanics, which operated the equipment, were complicated and needing calibrating to perfection so a test would be carried out.

On the morning the watch would change and two local officers took over.

Alongside the bed was a bookcase, this would slide and behind it was the chamber of execution. All the dignitaries would be present and the actual operation was very swift.

How true it was I don't know, but it was rumoured that a hangman who smoked cigars would leave his cigar on the shelf at the top of the boardroom fireplace and return in time to pick it up without marking the shelf.

True or not, I think I have covered enough of this subject and we will move on to brighter times.

Although the type of work we do is of a serious nature, it does have its compensations and sometimes produces comical interludes – Some are quickly forgotten but I have tried to provide a flavour throughout the book of some that readily spring to mind.

One such incident happened at Birmingham. A prisoner who had been sent to us for some reason or other had his mail re-directed from his previous prison – like others he eagerly awaited news from the home front.

He was issued with this letter, which he started reading and as he read, so his temperament changed and by the time he had completed reading he threw down his tray and stormed off from the servery and returned to his cell.

In the afternoon after he had calmed down we enquired what the cause of his tantrum was?

His explanation proved amusing to us but definitely not to him. At his previous prison, his cell overlooked a block of houses and one bedroom was occupied by his wife, who to maintain personal contact was undressing at the window for him nightly. There was however one small problem, he did not occupy the cell because he had been spirited away to us.

It transpired that she had been giving her nightly floorshow for the benefit of – not her husband – but an old dosser who must have had his day made.

I'm sure that had he made contact with the true husband – his days would have been numbered and that would have been his last floorshow.

Blow Ups

A violent situation could erupt at any time, one moment you are engaged in a rational conversation and the next, for no apparent reason, he has blown his top and begins lashing out at anyone who unfortunately just happens to be around.

Maybe the cause is a flash back from past encounters, who knows? I know one thing for certain, at times like this extreme care is needed when dealing with these characters, because to say that they are volatile is an understatement.

Once a well-known prisoner when going out to his morning exercise – hung back mumbling that I had better look in a certain cell where I would discover something intended for me.

Whilst the prisoner in this cell was out on his exercise my colleague and I searched the cell. We found a bandage rolled tightly into a circle and a piece to fit over the hand – harmless you may say – but embedded into it and secured were many pieces of jagged broken glass, which certainly wouldn't have done any one much good cosmetically.

We took immediate possession of this evil object and the man eventually was moved to a special hospital – our job was bad enough, but I do not envy the staff at these hospitals theirs either. Anyhow I remain eternally grateful to that prisoner.

On another search we found a large hacksaw blade, sharpened with an evil point - another vicious piece of weaponry – remember, I said that they had twenty four hours each day to outwit us and everything happened when you least expected it. We just had to try to be one step ahead at all times.

One notorious character around whom a TV programme was based had a reputation for violence and was always around when trouble was brewing. Obviously, he ended up on the block and under our charge. For some reason, best known to himself, the Governor directed that this man be allowed to sit outside of his cell for a certain period on a daily basis. We introduced one condition, which was that if an alarm bell should ring he would return to his cell and slam the door.

Strangely, the testing of alarm bells would take place just as he sat down outside the cell. Upon hearing this he would run into his cell pushing the door shut. He never asked to come out again and quite content to have been afforded the privilege, settled down.

Funny how they view a sense of loyalty – One day he approached me asking for a cardboard box to keep his girlfriends letters in. Thinking nothing of this I found him one. This served to help me on two occasions in the future, both times when he had barricaded his cell up and refusing to come out. After speaking with him he came out very easily because, as he put it! I had kept my word when I found him a box. Strange where loyalties lie isn't it. Who would imagine that an item as simple as a cardboard box would save a violent situation!

One other task was to issue, soap, tooth powders and razor blades to each wing P.O. The blades would be one and a fraction of a blade to each prisoner per week. The P.O. in question tried to make me issue him an extra blade so he was able to shave daily – reluctantly – or so I told him I had to refuse his request because of accountability. This wasn't the real reason – he was the person who tried to drop me in it when the Governor came to adjudicate and caught someone smoking – that someone was the P.O. but you will remember he blamed me. They say revenge is sweet and this time it certainly was.

LIGHT INTERLUDES

Dons Marine

Amongst the many talents prisoners possessed, we had a particular one who was a very good model maker. His skill was doll making – especially military uniforms.

One of our Principal Officers was an ex Royal Marine and he persuaded this prisoner to make him a doll attired in R.M. dress. This doll took pride of place and stood in the centre of a small polished table. It was cleverly crafted and was his pride and joy.

On this particular morning we stood at the ready to unlock, when an angry yell echoed around the prison. Slowly the reason emerged and the grins began to appear on many faces.

The doll was in his usual position sited on the table, but was standing inside the dirtiest plastic chamber pot imaginable.

The air became blue and remained so for the whole of that day. I think that most of us used discretion and kept well away from the Centre P.O.

This was not the only thing of his, which was sabotaged that day. On his wall hung a print of one of the ships that he had served on. Someone had also stuck cut-outs of German aircraft dive bombing the ship. – Not me! But again he was not too pleased.

He presented the evidence to the Governor of the day, but the Governor didn't seem over concerned, because he was an ex-Black Watch Officer and dare I suggest, that a friendly rivalry existed between the various sections of the armed forces. Later in the day a group of senior staff were laughing heartily and I'm sure that this was the result of the Governor relating the tale to his colleagues.

Having a sense of humour was essential in a job where close co-operation was so important but so was keeping practical jokes in proportion.

*Laugh If You Dare

The Chief Officer's office was situated on the centre and being an old prison, the room was blessed with a large open fireplace. In cold weather it was lit giving out a cheery feeling. I might add the only cheery feeling that ever came from the Chief's office.

This particular morning I was standing on the landing directly above the Chief's office. The prison was beginning to come to life when all of a sudden a heck of a commotion came from the direction of the Chief's office. We started to make our way down in case the Chief was in trouble. Suddenly the door burst open and out he came, his normally brilliant white shirt was black, as was his face. He yelled at me, words to the effect that if I so much as dared to grin, then I would be placed on a charge. Naturally I kept a straight face, although my stomach ached with wanting to burst out laughing. Later I had my laugh, but not in earshot of him.

It transpired that whilst he was checking print outs of the night time clocks a large crow had visited via the chimney, flapping around and depositing soot all over the office and his shirt. I shouldn't think that his good lady was very happy when he presented himself for his breakfast later that morning wearing a less than white shirt.

Such comments from his more senior colleagues were, "Looks a bit black over Bill's Mother's Chief," or "Lots of black clouds around today Chief," but simply not appreciated by him and like Queen Victoria he was not amused.

---

* See illustration nine "Laugh if you dare"

MORE ROUTINE

Mealtimes

I have indicated how vulnerable and explosive meal times could be and just to help this along even more, each prisoner was issued with a compartmentalised steel tray. Yes, a very handy weapon for the disgruntled diner, not only this, but the careless or even deliberate server could quite easily mix the gravy with the sweet or custard on the cabbage. Neither of which were very appetising.

This happened many times and the end result was the tray being at best thrown on the floor and at worst over someone's head, including staff. I think that I am safe now by saying that it never happened to me. Fortunately a different system is being used with much safer utensils at many prisons. They can still throw them should they wish but with less devastating effects than the edge of a steel tray. Food has also improved considerably with the choice of two or three main courses. The modern prison service! I dread to think of the reaction of some of the old timers who ruled with a rod of iron.

Those days prisoners expected and asked for nothing more than what they were entitled to. Not today! However, this is the age of the thinking prisoner. Many of the older element still prefer the old system. As they put it, "At least we knew where we stood" and maybe they have got a point.

Censorship

Only under certain circumstances may prisoner's mail be censored i.e. on the direction of a prison governor. If a prisoner represents a threat or danger to the police, public or state especially because of the nature of the crime or it could be that he was suspected of making escape plans.

One item of mail that is rarely allowed to be censored is mail to or from a legal advisor and then only in very exceptional circumstances.

When staff read mail they are trained to skim through the contents and only if it becomes blatantly obvious that something is not quite correct do they read it more deeply. There is a definite art to censoring and usually any suspect contents are quickly sifted out. Often staff are misrepresented as being insensitive. The majority of staff I have worked with are just the opposite, very caring people.

Despite the care taken, censorship has been seen as an intrusion into people's private affairs and much relaxation has recently taken place. In many circumstances letters are handed directly to the prisoner without even being checked. In some ways this method respects people's privacy but being from the old school I found that much information could be gleaned by casting a professional eye over the contents of a letter, for example, indicators of mood swings which may be caused through worries or pressures. Letters could give hints that a prisoner had either had intention of harming himself or indeed harming others or of escaping. Incoming letters could give information relating to a death or illness in the family or other domestic problems and staff would then be prepared to expect changes in patterns of behaviour of usually well behaved prisoners such as sudden anger outbursts, moods of depression or using violence. Being aware will help them decide on which is the best course of action. Sometimes all that is required is a sympathetic ear and to be able to talk and relieve the tension.

So, bearing all this in mind relaxing the censorship rule is perhaps a retrograde step because no one is aware of bad news or problems until it is too late.

Sometimes prisoners would deliberately make a derogatory remark about an officer or mislead staff by putting false information in a letter about a supposed illegal activity. Hoping to lead them onto a wild goose chase or set up a diversion, but mainly the situation was balanced and prisoners accepted censorship as a part of a normal prison regime.

Searching

I do not believe in predictability when dealing with a subject as vitally important as this.

It is part of our insurance policy and if anyone has something to hide then it is intended for an illegal act. I agree that some are comparatively harmless, such as tobacco or money. However it can be argued that even these two items can be used to purchase something that could endanger lives.

Escape equipment and weapons are amongst the most important items to locate and it is for this reason that searching plays such a vital part in day to day prison control.

I feel that some searches should be allowed to be conducted at any time of the day or even night. If it is telegraphed to the population then they will take evasive action and quickly dispose of any illegal items.

In prison several types of searches are carried out, amongst which the most regular is known as a 'rub down' search. This is a quick, but thorough on the spot search usually used when prisoners are being moved from one place to another, i.e. from a workshop to a visit, or from a cell to the segregation unit. A special search is what it implies and can only be conducted on authorisation of a higher rank for a special purpose. For instance, if a prisoner is suspected of carrying a weapon or an illegal item such as a bulk amount of money or escape equipment, i.e. a hacksaw blade. Cell searches are carried out more on a routine basis. This is when every item is checked in the prisoner's cell, including the cell furniture, bedding and belongings.

Workshops are regularly searched and this is a massive task with obviously a million hiding places.

Once a search we conducted revealed plans and handcuff keys neatly hidden wrapped in a rag and pushed down a tubular scaffold pole. Like looking for a proverbial needle in a haystack it was just that Lady Luck was on our side this time.

Rumour had it that a gun in parts was circulating in one large prison I worked in. I have no doubt this was genuine because a Churchill Tank could be hidden in the vast area of some prisons, let alone a small handgun.

While searching, you would always be aware of hidden dangers, for example, on a 'rub down' search officers started at the arms and the collar of a jacket. There were very dangerous hiding places because pieces of blade or darning needles made a nasty mess if you were not prepared and they were secreted in between the coat lapels.

I am confident that we did not find everything that was hidden, yes we found some and we did at least create a deterrent and this is why I feel searching would be of more benefit were it at random times and unannounced. If this had to be carried out during the small hours or Sunday afternoons it is always well to remember that often it is someone's physical well being, possibly life that we are playing with and sometimes it could be ones own life. Who knows?

Visits

Visits also play a very important part in prisoners' lives, especially their domestic visits, which help to maintain the link between family and friends and keep the prisoner in touch with the outside world. There were very few who didn't eagerly look forward to visiting day.

The visit was a very sensitive occasion and could often lead to angry outbursts especially if a few home truths were told. Staff had to handle each situation extremely carefully and although on the constant watchout for trouble or attempts at handing over unauthorised items they tried to keep a discreet distance.

Every visit needed 'kid glove' treatment, because it didn't take much to create a flashpoint especially if emotions were running high.

I have seen staff who innocently made remarks just to be sociable become the brunt of someone's frustrations and other staff having to intervene in an attempt to smooth over a nasty situation.

Confrontation didn't happen all of the time and many used to enjoy friendly banter with staff. Experience showed when and where not to say anything.

During visits constant vigilance had to be maintained in the rooms where they were taking place. Many methods were employed to hand items to prisoners. Examples were – by kissing and whilst in close contact an item, say a £5.00 note would be transferred from one mouth to another.

If we saw this we would immediately engage the suspect in continual conversation. It is extremely hard to talk with an item concealed in your mouth and eventually they would have to spit it out.

A serious attempt would be to swallow the object relating mainly to drugs in a contraceptive and passing it through the body when going to the toilet. If this was suspected the prisoner would be segregated and his motions examined until the offending article passed. This job usually fell to hospital officers. Not one I envied them doing.

Hospital officers were initially trained to be general disciplinary prison officers but had decided to specialise in the nursing field. First, they would have to attend a very comprehensive course and pass exams, the course spanning about two years.

This attracted a wide range of people, some of whom were ex-civilian nurses or medics in the services but also many who had no previous experience whatsoever, coming from mining or industry others from clerical backgrounds. Often the non-experienced staff turned out to be excellent hospital staff. Not only were they trained in the modern concepts of nursing but also were very able to relate to prisoners on an even footing.

Much of hospital work involved dealing with prisoners undergoing medical or mental observations, who it was found would place complete trust in someone such as an hospital officer, but be suspicious of a uniformed discipline officer. In those days we all wore white short coats whilst in the prison but prisoners were still able to distinguish between hospital and general duties staff.

When I refer to strange patterns of behaviour I am talking about the minority because the majority of prisoners just wish to serve their sentence and get out as soon as possible.

At the end of visits each prisoner would be given a search and close observations had to be kept because with large numbers of prisoners and visitors intermingling, anything could happen, especially passing items over.

We also tried to keep prisoners who had been searched apart from those who hadn't because it would be easy to pass illegal items over to those who had passed through the searching routine. These prisoners would face very little risk of being searched again unless they were under further suspicion.

The rightful owner on their next meeting would then retrieve the item and a small payment made for their trouble.

Long Lost Friends

People returning to prison would often greet staff like long lost friends and when the subject of their return was referred to they would reply in on of two ways :- By a roundabout admission – "Well you know what it's like Guv! – A few drinks and everything looked so easy and like a fool I fell for it" or, "I was fitted up" usually casting the blame towards the police. Hardly ever true but one particularly strange case was when a man serving a relatively long sentence accused a police officer of planting explosive equipment in the same house as his baby. He continually bore a grudge and swore vengeance but nothing came of the threats. However, he did manage to get two enquiries instituted by independent police authorities and both finding no case to answer in respect of his allegations.

Regimes were strict and prison rules enforced rigidly. Longer-term prisoners were able, as they progressed through their sentences to earn extra privileges. For example, the majority of prisoners were restricted to eating meals in their cells, but 'Stage prisoners,' as long termers were known, were allowed to dine in association in the mess. They could watch T.V. or play indoor games such as table tennis, pool or board games - Staff had to be on the look out for gambling which I am sure took place. Some of them would bet everything. It could be the first (screw) prison officer to enter the room to who would win the 1.30 pm at Ascot.

This is where debts would build up and the rough stuff would start.

They were also allowed 'Stage Papers,' national newspapers which others had to buy.

Many of the training prisoners for long termers were well away from their homes and it was for this reason they were allowed to accumulate their domestic visits for 12 months and return to the nearest prison to their home and take all visits say in a two week period. The only stipulation was that they were required to abide by the local prisons rules.

These 'Stagers' were seen by their younger admirers as something like cult figures. I remember one whose claim to fame was that he had received both the 'birch' and the 'cat of nine tails,' neither of which he was proud of and didn't hesitate to warn others of the consequences of this. A man of very small stature – makes one wonder how he could cause the violence that he did.

Communications

In prison the occupants devised many of their own methods to communicate with others when they were locked up.

Commonly a system used was tapping the heating pipes, which echoed along the landing operating to a code similar to Morse. This was effective if solely operated between two people, but this didn't always work out as planned because others joined in and completely sabotaged the entire system. Shouting from cell to cell wasn't a wise idea for two reasons: Space was limited and cell bars restricted people's ability to get their heads out to talk freely. The conversations could be over heard by anyone else, including prison staff.

The favoured method was 'the line.' A prisoner wishing to convey a message to another would suspend a line made usually of thread smuggled out from the mailbag shop. This would be weighted with the message attached and swung in a pendulum motion until it reached the intended person. Sometimes it would be an article like tobacco or someone disposing of an illicit item expecting to be searched. Again, this system was fraught with problems because someone else may also be on the lookout and intercept the package – especially tobacco – before it reached the person for whom it was intended. The task to trace the culprit would more or less be impossible.

There was no method which was foolproof except by direct contact and at that time a policy was in being to segregate the various classes of prisoner - Adult from young offender - convicted from non-convicted and * star prisoners from those who had served previous sentences. Like many other things the prisoners found a way around this and would you believe that the church provided this avenue. On Sundays communal church services were held and all categories converged in the chapel. The policy of segregation was still enforced but to assist the Chaplain was a

---

* First Adult Sentence

prisoner orderly, who amongst his many other jobs would hand hymn and prayer books to each prisoner.

This is where the communication took place. If say a convicted prisoner wished to communicate with a remand prisoner, he would write out his message, which would be placed in between the leaves of the book and issued to the prisoner. The Chapel orderly took a risk and if caught would lose his own job so he charged a price. The other way was by singing the message in the hymn. Fairly safe systems! But once again the exception provided the rule, more than once a singing message was passed on to a worshipping member of staff and intended incidents were averted.

One Sunday the chapel orderly was called off at short notice for a police visit. Unfortunately, it was around the time hymn book were to be issued. The Chaplain stepped into the breach in his good hearted Christian manner distributing the books to the wrong people; consequently the messages were passed to the wrong people. The chapel orderly then became an unpopular character because prisoners had paid in advance for the service. Fortunately for him he was whisked off to await further charges, because had he have returned the consequences would have been dire.

No positive guarantee could be given that messages would reach their intended destination but being who they were and being where they were, they would continue to try every conceivable method at their disposal.

The System

In days past the system rarely concerned itself with rehabilitation. Officers who saw this as a useful area of treatment were in the minority and frowned upon by their more senior colleagues, who believed that prisoners were in for punishment and not as punishment these were known as "The hang em! Flog em! Brigade." The outlook has now turned full circle and concentrates on Prison Rule 1 which says, that the object of imprisonment is to send a person out of prison better than when they came in and to encourage them to lead a good and useful life when they are released.

So how was this achieved? From the day after their reception, prisoners were seen by an observation and classification unit, who would decide the best form of treatment for each individual and where they should serve their sentence. A prisoner receiving a sentence of life imprisonment would probably need a much more in depth plan than those serving just months would. The unit would assess the particular needs for each individual, taking into account their educational ability and skills. They would also look at where individuals would gain the most benefit; one person may require basic needs such as education and work but another, maybe at an advanced level of education or professional skills, both serving sentences but both requiring an entirely different training plan.

Even from the day of reception, plans for discharge and resettlement were being formed. The person receiving advanced education may, in fact be homeless or have a bad domestic situation where as the person requiring basic skills could have a perfectly settled home life with no problems, so plans have to be tailored to suit each individuals requirements.

Great emphasis is placed on education, especially evening classes and further education, computer skills and art being amongst the most popular.

The Mountbatten Report

In 1969 an enquiry was set up headed by Lord Louis Mountbatten following certain sensitive escapes involving two great train robbers. A spy and a member of the London underworld. It also looked into re-shaping prison systems, staffing levels, shift patterns and the promotion structure. The report, known as 'The Mountbatten Report' made 52 recommendations.

It recommended that prisons used UHF radio and staff were to be trained in its operation. Dogs were to be brought into security prisons and that handlers were trained by police to their standards. That closer liaison between prison and police existed, especially when prisoners were being escorted outside jails.

It also created a new rank, that of Senior Officer, equivalent probably to that of a Police Sergeant. The latter being well overdue.

The report clearly worded and made very interesting reading. Out of the recommendations some were not adopted. It recommended that a prison should be built on the Isle of Wight to house longer-term prisoners. The regime would be fairly liberal inside but the outside would be sort of a fortress and virtually impregnable. He recommended Vectis after the old name of the island.

One of the most important recommendations was re-classifying prisoners into one of the four categories explained below.

Category (A) Were top security, if they escaped, they would be a danger to the police or the public or an embarrassment to the state. These people possessed the financial backing to be able to effect an escape and were to be very carefully controlled and every movement accounted for.

Category (B) Were people who could fall within the category A area but did not have the financial resources, so were not seen as such a danger, although again they were closely supervised.

Category (C) Were just normal run of the mill prisoners not much danger but not quite ready for the lowest category.

Category (D) Were considered as suitable for open conditions and needed minimum supervision in a fairly open regime where much was based on self trust. However, a category D could rapidly revert to a C even a B if circumstances changed i.e. a domestic break up or faced with further charges.

Another recommendation Mountbatten made was to set up a network of control rooms within prisons and to train staff to operate them. Thus co-ordinating the movement of the various departments and paying particular attention to dog patrols and outer security patrols giving them instant contact in the event of an emergency. Also creating a link to both divisional police and the main police information rooms.

Once again, I shook off the return to general discipline duties because I was destined to join the control room team. Initially as a relief chasing all over the prison changing batteries, earning the nickname 'Goffer,' changing sets if they didn't work. Many didn't because we ended up with a lot of the police 'cast-offs,' then eventually I joined the main team.

The introduction of radio caused great hilarity amongst the inmate population and cartoons began to appear, especially depicting two cocoa tins and thread. We needed to stabilise the situation and came up with a plan.

One morning as we walked the grounds testing the sets – a group of prisoners started uttering derogatory comments. The officer dug into his pocket producing a 'Swan Vestas' matchbox into which he stuck a pencil. Talking into this contraption he created great hilarity amongst the troops who thought that he had gone mad until a voice echoed that he had been received 'loud and clear.' Many prisoners stood open mouthed as the officer, unconcerned slowly removed the pencil from the matchbox and replaced both items into his pocket. The smart alecs had been played at their own game and we had won. The truth was that we had played a perfectly timed hoax. Arrangements had been made that at a certain time control would speak to the outstation who had the receiver secreted on him with volume turned up so anyone could hear.

It worked like clockwork and it was a long while before they realised the joke had been on them and when they did they were conspicuous by their absence.

The Control Room plotted movements of prisoners and the whereabouts of dog handlers and other patrols ensuring their safety.

Whilst on the subject of dogs being introduced, not only did the inmate population steer clear but also the wild cats began to dwindle. They didn't go far however, because they started to congregate in the prison and around the landings. Work in the Control Room was interesting with plenty to organise. Unfortunately it involved a lot of nights when incidentally most of the incidents happened – incidents such as escape attempts, cell smash ups and sickness – at such times the prison was only as physically safe as a depleted staff made it. Sounds and their location were very difficult to locate exactly and differing sounds became magnified and eerie without any indication of where they were coming from.

Talking of sounds, one night duty, during which we patrolled the landings wearing plimsolls or slippers in case you disturbed the guests. I was walking around on the upper landings, which was an ablutions area in which was positioned centrally a galvanised rubbish bin. As I passed, a resident pigeon took off from the bin sending the bin lid clattering to the floor disturbing many of the prisoners which did not go down at all well at two thirty in the morning. Prisoners were shouting and banging, being unconvinced that it wasn't the screws doing it deliberately to get their own back, as for me, it scared the living daylights out of me. I think it took most of the night for me to recover from the shakes, as for the other staff they thought the episode to be hilarious and it remained the talking point for the remainder of the shift.

In the Control Room we worked alone and an uneventful shift could be extremely boring. The dog patrol staff used to visit for a chat and during one of these chats the handler was standing outside talking and enjoying a drink, his dog was seated, and all of a sudden the dog let out a tremendous yell and leapt into the air. It transpired that he had seated himself on the top of a rat hole and as the rat emerged finding something blocking his exit bit the rear of the dog. I think I may well have taken off, don't you?

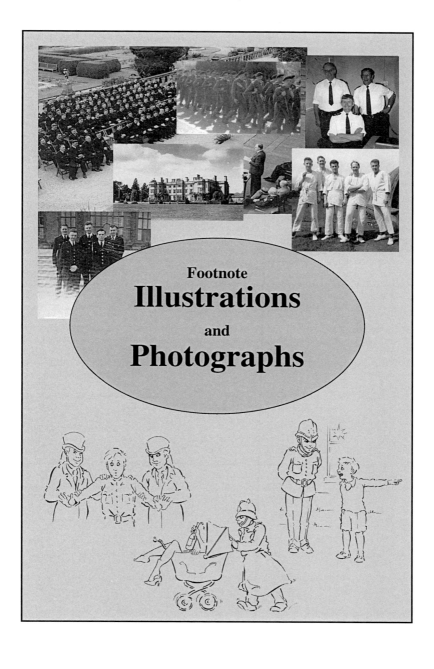

Footnote
Illustrations
and
Photographs

"I've come for the body"

"Oh, you've got a handle to your name"

"Looking somewhat like a billiard ball"

"Walks up to the dustcart and
smartly salutes"

"Luck played a big part"

"I didn't paint any car mister"

"Quickly thinking he handed the baby
to the young officer and deposited the
woman in the pram"

"All of a sudden the doors burst open
and in came a large contingent of staff"

"Laugh if you dare"

"If I make one sir will I still get my promotion"

"Someone had nailed up the door
despite the protests"

OH MY, WHAT A CLEVER DOGGIE YOU HAVE YOUNG MAN!

"Closeting chain"

Anyone for a walk?
Army style

Eynsham Hall police
training college

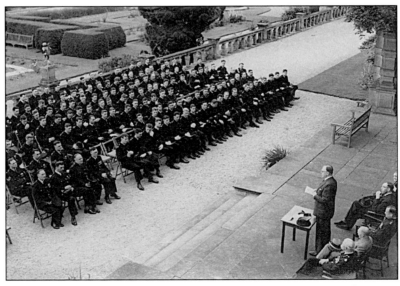

The Home Secretary addresses us on our passing out parade

365 Squad Royal Military Police 1953

The author with his new wife

A few of us on the
college steps

Attired for judo

The author with two of his
senior staff at Sudbury

The author

Jacobean-style
Prison

Typical Victorian
Prison Gates

Typical Modern Security
Prison Gates

HMP Kennet entrance, the
latest prison to open

Sudbury by Photographs . . .

Entrance to H.M.P. Sudbury

Administrative Centre

New accommodation

Laundry Operation

Lawns & Gardens fronting Administrative Centre

Propagating Centre Entrance to H.M.P. Sudbury

The bowling green at Sudbury

The visiting area at Sudbury

The Chapel interior

The author on his retirement as
Commissionaire at Devonshire House

THANKS TO LORD LOUIS

A Step Up

Having outlined the Mountbatten Report as mentioned relating to the introduction of an intermediate rank. By good fortune I fitted the requirement and applied to take the vocational exam. The position offered two inroads, one by having served 7 years and taking the exam, the avenue I went and the other having served 10 years and attending an interview.

As we walked away from the centre one candidate remarked, "Only an idiot would fail that exam" – He failed!

On the day the results came out we knew that only seven had passed and as the day passed by six of the successes had been advised and there were a number awaiting the outcome. Nail biting time!

I was working a late shift and at 10.00 pm my relief arrived, dejectedly I walked to the Gate Lodge to hand in my keys, when I was told that the Governor wished to see me. I entered his office to be greeted by, "Well are you going to take it again?" I replied, "I would." He said, "You won't have to bother because you've passed."

I drove home on cloud nine. An outcome that I saw as important on reflection was not so important because ones family should take a far greater priority.

This wasn't the end however, because we had to apply for a promotion board and it was not certain that you would be considered and even being called, at least two thirds would still fail.

I was lucky however and on a bleak November day on route to the interview I passed Westminster Abbey where a funeral parade was taking place for a famous Second World War air ace. Standing watching, fascinated, I felt that I was attending my own and suddenly jolted myself with the thought that if I didn't get a move on I would be late. Usual board, usual questions – a nice guy a hard nut and a mediator.

My post mortem on the return journey said I could go either way. Lady Luck shone on me that day and I was recommended for promotion and on top of that I only had two weeks to wait before I received my posting to Onley Borstal Recall Centre.

BOYS INSIDE

Onley – A New View

It was only a matter of weeks before I was informed that I was to be transferred to Onley Borstal recall Centre in the new grade.

Onley was near to Rugby in Warwickshire and centrally poised to receive intakes from prisons throughout Britain. Although I was looking forward to climbing the ladder there was three snags.

All staff wore civilian clothes. Having worn a uniform all through my previous services I wondered if this would cause any untoward problem, it didn't.

The person in charge did not recognise the rank of senior officer and any overtime obtainable would have to be by working in the lower grade, i.e. supervision of groups of boys, either in a workshop or on an outside working party. Some of the staff had no option because of financial pressure. I did it once with some of the most difficult boys I had met, afterwards I vowed that I would only accept to cover my own grades absences. Eventually this was agreed and the new grade recognised but before this fate took a turn.

Mountbatten's report stated that two way radio was to be introduced into all establishments, but had not yet reached Onley. Having had previous experience I was selected to attend an instructors course at Ham Common in Surrey. Following this, to teach the staff the correct procedures and its operation. Also it was added that overtime would be involved and after discussion it was agreed that the rate would be as a Senior Officer. This opened the floodgates and all Senior Officer grades claimed higher rates of pay for overtime which was changed to cover absences in their own grade and higher grades. This helped, not only from the financial point but also in gaining experience of the higher-grade duties.

I was disrupting my wife by making her move again. This to me was the most important problem and one I should have considered more seriously. On reflection I had my priorities wrong – promotion was no where near as important as home life.

The situation of wearing civilian clothes meant that the boys did not see you as being any different from any other member of staff and the only respect you got was only the respect you earned. Easier said than done.

It was once summed up by two boys I was walking with: – In the distance was a coach bringing a new intake from a prison in London and supervising its unloading was a number of uniformed prison officers. The comment made by one boy to the other was "Effing screws". I intervened by pointing out that I was one of those so-called screws, to which the other boy said, "Oh, no sir you are a borstal officer, which is entirely different." He would not accept that we were all member of the same prison service.

Borstal Recall meant that after a boy had served a sentence of Borstal training, he would be released for six months or the unexpired portion of his sentence which ever was the greater. If he got into further trouble during this period the court could return him to Borstal by having him recalled. The other way he could be recalled was by breaching terms of his licence. For example, refusing to report to the Borstal After Care Officers or not attending work which had been found for him, plus numerous other rules and regulations.

The majority of boys were aged between fifteen and twenty-one but I've known boys, men of twenty-four.

One of these had served abroad in the army and it wasn't until three years later he returned and was arrested and recalled to Borstal, but only for a short spell. He did, as I understand return to the army and made a success of it.

A target date was usually around seventeen weeks, some more, some less, depending on various circumstances relating mostly to re-settlement and the domestic position. Much of this was dependent on the review boards. This is where the boys began to recognise that we had some considerable power in determining release dates, where by having their future in our hands.

Boys who were allocated a date a little later than a mate for a variety of reasons became very upset and on a number of occasions aggressive, despite the fact that they would more than likely commit further offences and be back inside again.

Keen Competition

We tried to create a competitive regime and each week a shield in the shape of a phoenix – the mythical bird, which rose from the ashes – was awarded to the best wing. The award was based on behaviour and achievement in the boys sporting, working and living pursuits. The award was coveted and was a real feather in the cap of the wing receiving it.

In addition to this we ran a wing competition and awarded a prize to the boys with the best-kept room. Daily, all rooms would be inspected and marks up to five given, points being deducted for any fault being found. The only danger being, that once a boy got his cell up to a high standard, then it was much easier to maintain and if we were not careful the same boy could win week after week. We had to find even the smallest of faults to stop this and the contortions the inspecting officer got into to find the fault were strange to say the least. Sometimes he had to be 'indiarubber'.

Nearly all the rooms were immaculate; those that weren't paid the penalty!

In borstal a facility existed whereby the wing housemaster dealt with minor breaches of discipline and any dirty types came under this umbrella.

A favourite with the boys was "Top of the Pops" on television. A pin could be heard and the dreaded punishment was to receive one nights no association on a Thursday, the night it was screened.

The threat of, "Don't forget it's Top of the Pops tonight" worked wonders on the Parade Square or at the boys workplace.

Should someone try to disrupt them, then they could watch out for repercussions from their own peer group. Care had to be taken that the stronger element did not take over and as every group has a leader we had to ensure that the leader was one of us.

Daddies

As prison had the 'baron', so the borstal had the 'daddy', same type but by a different name. There were some very strong characters. Once, whilst working on the punishment block we had one of these characters located and after talking to him he volunteered a full statement, exposing some of the rackets they practised. Amongst these was a weekly raffle. Everyone except the very strongest was forced to take part and contribute 10p. The borstal held over 300, so quite an amount of money was exchanging hands. The boys were p[aid in cash and were permitted to hold up to one and a half times their earnings, so there was no difficulty extracting the monies.

The twist came when the prize was awarded to some insignificant individual who would receive 50p. The wing Daddies would share the remainder out, £29 not bad for an evenings work.

I enquired as to how they could guarantee the winner being the person they wished it to be. The answer was simple. Every name in the hat was the same. Clever really, it's just a pity they didn't make schemes like that work outside. Or did they?

The borstal was said to be run on a public school system, discipline was strict and the emphasis besides compulsory education was to pack the days full of activity.

Pressed Men

Partaking in sport was compulsory, not only for the boys but also the staff were included.

I was given the volleyball and some of the most obnoxious characters one would wish to meet. The boy who had the ball tried to hit it into the sky as high as possible, followed by many claps and cheers. 'Watch it' I though or this will get out of hand. So I gave a warning – to be ignored – "The next one is nicked" I said and he was followed by another. The Governor backed me and awarded appropriate punishments. This helped because eventually I managed to find the boys interested in the serious game, they formed a very good team taking the local volley ball league title. I found that with these characters you couldn't just make loose threats, you had to show you meant business. I recall another time when an officer had to charge a youth with assault during a basketball competition. What better time to get their own back – despite his protestations he was convicted.

Meals were served in the wing dining rooms by a team of boys and staff. Usually the atmosphere was good with supervising staff walking around and chatting at the tables. The conversations could range from anything from football to sorting out their own worries or settling an argument. Of course sometimes the situation turned nasty but you could usually detect the build up to this by the attitudes shown.

It may be absolute silence, but looking daggers at each other, or on the other hand it maybe a full-scale argument that suddenly breaks into a fight.

I found boys very much motivated by trying to act out the actions of their favourite T.V. hard men. They see their heroes take on the World and try to do the same.

Visits were very important to the boys – I say boys, but a large number were married with children.

Lies and Damn Lies.

Many is the time that they have boasted of Dads Jaguar and living a life of luxury only to see their poor parents struggling up the drive clutching a tattered old carrier. So much for their fantasies.

Whilst talking of fantasies I remember one boy being discharged to Coventry. This particular morning I received a letter saying how well he was doing only to be informed that he had died in a canoeing accident. The truth was that he had been fantasising that he was a brilliant swimmer and as such had been allowed on a canoe trip. The canoe capsized and he had drowned. The truth was he was not able to swim a stroke. So much for his fantasising which had cost him his life.

Back to visits and reunions. One so called 'Hard Man' visited by his mum swaggered into the visits room in front of his mates only to receive a sound smack round both ears from mum who previous to his arrival had been talking to his case officer who had been relating his progress or lack of it in this case. The boy burst into tears but was never quite the little hard man as he thought in front of his mates ever again – Summary jurisdiction!

Case work was a vital part of borstal management and progress reports from virtually every department were submitted by the staff prior to each review. They played a very important aid to the review board and they took the reports into account when deciding upon target dates for the boys' release.

Strangely enough there was no collusion but comments followed a very similar pattern good or bad. The man in the workshop, the chaplain and the physical education officer. Would probably reach a similar conclusion as the case officer despite the fact that they rarely came into contact with each other.

All Stations Change

Without much warning – except of course from the rumour factory the staff were notified that from a certain date the establishment would change into a closed Borstal for the violent type of offender.

From then we hadn't much time to organise the change. We visited various other closed Borstals to view the regimes and look at what could fit into our plans.

The time the boys would be with us would be much longer and it was thought that our target date would be around 42 weeks. So we had to introduce many changes to the training plans that we currently had in operation.

There were different sets of documentation to be used – Review board dates would change staff would be working much closer with a view to becoming more involved in caseworking.

A great emphasis was placed on learning a trade. The trades taught ranged from metal working to all aspects of building. A very popular course was the skilled labourer's course, which taught everything such a person would be required to do from basic bricklaying to woodwork.

Strangely enough a large number of boys to receive a borstal sentence or 'fresh whack' as they called it were boys we previously had as borstal recalls.

Staff would be expected to become more deeply involved by organising camping trips, visits to football matches and often taking them home to a meal. The policy was encouraged and frequently when discharged, letters would be exchanged between a case officer and his charges.

When some of the boys came in they were aggressive and anti-social but by the time they went out they were responsive and co-operative. This gave staff satisfaction and a feeling of achievement.

For a boy to try to put one over another's case officer was a cardinal sin in the boys' eyes and woe betide anyone trying it out. To this end the boys showed a strange sense of loyalty.

During my spell at Onley I spent a period in charge of the punishment wing most of the boys who entered this area were charged with either fighting or assault. Many acting out their fantasies especially those involving their favourite T.V. or film heroes. Violence is not new but it seems that there was less weaponry used or carried.

What is the answer no one really knows but my personal opinion is that the abolition of National Service was a huge mistake. To a certain extent I kicked at the system but when I realised that each time the system would be the winner I settled down learning to obey orders. The borstal boys especially the 18-20 year olds would most probably not have been borstal boys because National Service would have intervened at the most crucial time.

Unlike the adult block I found the borstal punishment system much more demanding, the occupants were always playing up, smashing up or barricading they lived in little worlds of their own and were always making demands.

This coupled with other pressures built up and one day it hit me like a sledgehammer. Suddenly I snapped. I was immediately seen by the Medical Officer and sent off sick.

I did not see this coming unlike my loved one and was unable to do justice to an excellent meal that day my wife had prepared. I was off work for sometime and that day virtually slept the clock round. From then onwards I vowed that I would never allow work to worry me to that extent ever again. This is a common place illness now and is called stress. This can kill.

Later in my service I trained and talked to many staff about 'Stress Management'. I think the real experience helped me to put the subject over with feeling. During much of our time in the wings we were absolutely snowed under with paper work or attending meetings which limited our time to carrying out our real job of dealing with people. To know people you must communicate and it is equally as important to be able also to listen.

As time didn't allow us to do what we would wish we found that the best way to get to know the boys was to find out which was their favourite leisure pursuit and join them at it. For many it was sports. Once you had their confidence they would talk much more easily than in the confines of an office. Even more so if the person talking to them was good at a game, which they were interested in. It was for this reason that we tried to fit officers who had the ability to play. Most of the boys were interested in football but for some it was table tennis, darts or snooker. Just sitting with them in a quiet room allowing them to talk revealed much.

Excused Prisoners

Eventually I was moved from wing work to staff detailing, this involved planning duties for all staff, covering all the necessary tasks, escorts and maintaining rosters. In addition to this you undertook duties of the higher grade as orderly officer. He visited all parts of the establishment ensuring all was well. He was a sort of trouble-shooter and dealt with everything no matter how large or how small.

Sometimes humour entered into the situation for example: - One lunchtime I received a phone call to say that an aeroplane had landed in the sports field. At first I thought it was a wind up by one of my colleagues because as you are no doubt finding out by now is that prison staff have a weird sense of humour. This was followed by another call from another wing repeating the same information. I was convinced by now this was a practical joke because I had heard nothing of an aeroplane but this was followed by a call from the Governor asking me to investigate and report back so I knew it was not a joke. It wasn't – on the sports field was a full sized glider which had tried to use our tarmac parade ground for thermal to gain some height but he hadn't made it and had to land in our sports field. Fortunately no injuries were sustained and the clear up operation was quickly carried out. A case of cry wolf once too often which could quite easily have miss-fired.

At the end of evening classes we would stand in the corridor leading to the wings to try to eliminate 'horse play' because where ever groups of boys are, fooling about will occur and our presence helped to calm things down.

A group of boys approached, one obviously made a pointed comment about us so by way of routine we enquired what he had been doing? He replied "Nothing". We asked him to show us the work in his exercise book. He tried to refuse and became a little stroppy. We changed the request to an order and took possession of the book finding it to contain some strange drawings. Suddenly we saw more into this and agreed this could be some form of cocking mechanism for a gun. After further investigation he revealed that he was the designer and another boy was making the mechanism in a metal workshop. We only found what could have been component parts but I dread to think what the outcome could have been had their plans come to fruition.

Dirty Tricks

Once female office staff were being pestered by a series of anonymous abusive and indecent phone calls all on the internal system. The caller knew every girl by name and suspicion began pointing towards a member of staff but we hadn't a clue who. It was just that who else would know all the internal telephone numbers.

Eventually we decided that perhaps we were concentrating in the wrong area and could it possible be an inmate! If so how could he gain this knowledge. This was narrowed down to a very few boys, each of whom should be under constant supervision.

This left two, one who worked in the officers mess he was quickly ruled out because the supervision he received was equally if not more so than by staff. The cook would not let him out of her sight and there were no phones in the loo!

One party remained – a number of boys were responsible for cleaning the offices in the corridor but they should have been supervised. We decided to wait and watch.

We had warned the girls that should they receive one of these calls to keep the caller talking as long as possible and contact us by some alternative means. Most of them worked in communal offices.

One morning we received a complaint, the lady in question engaged the caller in conversation and a girl on another phone contacted us. Whilst she was doing this we entered the only possible office this could be taking place and lo and behold comfortably seated on the office table was the cleaner talking to someone, he tried to put the phone down but was not quick enough and after taking the handset we talked to the other person who was the complainant.

He looked somewhat annoyed at being disturbed but couldn't deny anything. He was charged internally and transferred for psychiatric assessment.

It was a quite simple how he found the girls names and extensions because above the phone in this office was a list of extensions and above each one was the Christian name of each girl. Simple, causing much tension and disruption between staff creating unfounded suspicion. Care was exercised in the future that all such lists were safely locked away from prying eyes and devious minds. They have all day to plot and plan and this is why I am all in favour of packing as much activity as possible into each day.

Everywhere I was stationed always produced one inmate who was much worse than any of the others and Onley was no exception. The boy I am calling to mind was constantly in trouble, mostly for silly offences but as it often is the case they progress from bad to worse. This young man attempted to burn the quiet room (the boys lounge) which could obviously have had a devastating effect. For this he was segregated but ordered to work – he refused. We were ordered to ensure that he was at work each day even if it meant carrying him and this is exactly what happened. He was carried to work deposited on a workbench collected at lunch returned and collected at cease labour – usually he just sat there. Often he would struggle and end up by falling in a puddle. He would remain sitting on a workbench most days. Eventually he was re-classified to adult status and left us – much to our delight not thinking of the receiving establishment's problem just glad to off load.

Another time an alarm bell sounded in the kitchen and upon attending was faced with a boy raising the alarm begging to be locked away from an extremely irate catering officer. I think this is the one and only time when I have known a prisoner pleading to be locked away from the wrath of staff, usually its the other way round.

The one character who no one wishes to meet is the nuisance – he is not exactly violent but can be but mainly he is constantly wanting and worrying. One of my Stoke friends summed up this character as a werrett – half worrier, half ferret.

All of the SO's used to be concerned about this type of character who could upset an entire wing without much of a problem. Some one however used to have them allocated and make the best of a bad job.

Being professional staff we would often spend more time with one of these boys than the others.

It was a sense of achievement if we were able to get them to comply with what were to you and I see as simple tasks such as bed making, cleaning your teeth or washing.

The reward for efforts came when the rough edges had been smoothed out; often they became a useful part of the wing population. Not always I might add.

As the orderly officer you took on board staff problems and like prisoners a few would let you down.

More Dirty Tricks.

One that I recall came to me with a sob story that his wife was ill and he needed to go off early. As it happened that evening due to one thing or another I was extremely short and one rule, which must never be broken, is to go below authorised safe manning levels. As he had a problem I decided to cover his job and sent him off early. Only the following morning to incur the wrath of the Chief. What had he done? Instead of going home he had visited the staff club, arming himself with a pint and settling down to a game of dominoes with his mate. Who should walk in – The Chief who enquired why he was not on duty – "Oh the Orderly Officer let me off"

Never again – he spoilt it for many of the others probably more genuine cases.

I saw him and advised him to never again to ask me for favours because refusal might offend.

One nasty one will stick in my memory forever. I had reported for duty one afternoon. The routine was to collect a radio and relieve the morning S.O. after he handed over any important information he would go off duty.

After he had left I received a call to go to the orderly room to sign an exchange of duty book. I did this and returned to prepare for the lads returning to work. Prior to this I unlocked my office but found my radio had vanished. I stopped all prisoner movement after checking if any of my staff had taken it and a full search was carried out by staff – No luck I reported the loss. I was charged with failing to carry the set and received a reprimand. This should stay on the record of service for seven years – My opinion is that it was always there.

*It was around the time when I had been selected for promotion and I became concerned that this breach would stand in my way. This was not to be the case because eventually I was promoted and posted. It did not go down at all well with me because prior to this my record was unblemished. One day whilst on leave from my new station I was shopping when I met up with my old boss and we sat down to a coffee because he advised me that he had something to tell me.

Apparently a prisoner had dropped a note in the box to say that if they wished to recover the radio taken from my locked office to look in the loft. True enough they found the radio but became suspicious as to the author of the note.

The person finding the note was instructed to submit a report. A number of senior staff compared handwriting and all came to the same conclusion – That both the notes and the report were written by the same person. It was never conclusively proved but with such a friend who needs enemies. This leaves a nasty taste in the mouth making one suspicious of everyone. I must stress however that despite such incidents, comradeship was normally very high.

---

* See illustration ten "If I make one sir will I still get my promotion"

Dirty Jokes

The boys were occupied in workshop or trade courses during the daytime and one shop was engaged in making up Christmas crackers. It won't take much to imagine what happened when the crackers were opened on the festive day – Girlie pictures fell out and some of the motifs and limericks wording was altered much to the hilarity of the boys and the embarrassment of the people who brought the crackers. Needless to say the contract was never renewed. I wonder why?

Young Prisoners

Towards the end of my seven years the establishment yet again changed its role and without too much warning became a prison for young offenders. Not too many staff were happy because any hope of rigid discipline was lost, as prison regimes were much more liberal as opposed to borstal and there were very few youngsters who didn't know their rights.

This change also lost us the civilian identity and all of us found ourselves in what was known as French Navy also differing badges of rank.

After seeing each other in civvies for years it was very hard to recognise one another in uniform. Most I identified by their style of walks. This made it easy for them to spot me because I tend to walk crow toed.

I had experienced three different regimes in seven years without moving but the latter one presented the hardest challenge.

One day I received a phone call from another wing enquiring if I needed any toilet rolls and not being one to refuse any reasonable offer I accepted. The person giving these away was not noted for his generosity and in hindsight I should have heard alarm bells ringing, however two boys trooped in dragging two mattress covers crammed full of the stuff. I put these away in our storeroom priding myself on this gain when the door opened and in walked the administration officer (a high grade civil servant) and said that he was going to carry out a check of surplus stores. When he saw my haul he went ballistic.

As for me I was not amused and at that moment in time would have willingly swung for my benefactor.

I received many calls during the afternoon from so called well wishers enquiring after my health and if my stomach had settled down etc. like Queen Vic I was not amused.

It was a rarity for girls to be accepted into a boy's borstal but there was always one exception to every rule.

My wife and I provided this exception when we arranged for our daughter to be christened in the chapel. The officiating vicar was affectionately known as "Mick the Vic". He was a down to earth man and in our view an ideal person to introduce our daughter into the ways of the Christian World. As for her she resented all this attention and started to make her point of view by crying, so much that I had to rapidly despatch her into an anti-room until she had quietened down.

This achieved I returned her into the chapel where she became a perfect little lady. After the proceedings my boss came over saying some of the truest words I have heard "Don't worry, they all go through these phases but they soon get out of them. The only problem they quickly go into another one which is usually worse". How true.

I have controlled men for most of my service but give me an angry man any time as opposed to the trials and tribulations of parenthood. Little girls have a charming but disarming manner of wheedling their way around Fathers. No, I wouldn't be without her!

Much has been written in the media relating to suicides and all due respect to the department who have laid down extremely strict procedures to be followed. I feel that if a person is sufficiently determined then no rules will ever stop them. Usually they are not the sort of person who broadcast their intentions to the World at large – just the opposite is the case the introvert who gives no sign whatsoever is the more likely person to do this. The attention seeker rarely carried out his threats and in my experience the only time this type succeeds is when the thing go wrong: - for example a cell fire which gets out of hand or a feeble attempt at slashing wrists which go to far.

Some of the boys were extremely impressionable and others gullible. For example at one period a group was formed by prisoners protecting their rights. It was widely publicised that a prisoners strike was on the cards and a date of non-co-operation fixed. We discussed this and decided not to take any action but to play the thing by ear.

The morning this was scheduled we entered the wing and unlocked the boys for our dining room and were greeted with the comment "I thought you were on strike today". We seized the opportunity and replied to the effect that we should have been but couldn't bear to see the boys locked away all day and out of the goodness of our hearts came in. The boys were delighted with this and we had no problems whatsoever.

I am sure that none of them realised that it was they who should have been on strike and not us.

Major incidents at this time were relatively rare however the occasional one did erupt.

This day we received information that a wing was about to erupt and all day we were tensed up expecting the worst. Nothing happened and as locking up time approached we were about to breathe a sigh of relief when the alarm bell rang. It came from the wing we expected it from. The boys had all refused to go into their cells. The adrenaline started to pump. Sixty to six not bad odds for them. We suggested that anyone who did not wish to be involved could go into their cells and push the doors to. To our relief the majority did literally that. I think that only two or three remained defiant but they were despatched to pastures new – rapidly.

Fortunately we had averted a potentially nasty situation but I can assure you it took ages to revert back to normal. I think that all of us were glad to be going off duty in one piece that night.

Before we changed to a uniformed establishment, I was sent to a top security prison in the aftermath of a riot along side other colleagues. We drove to the establishment Gartree Prison not knowing just what to expect. We all had one big problem we were in plain clothes. We arrived and after finding the others were whisked away I was taken to the Chiefs office and told that I had been temporarily promoted and given the job as Hiking P.O. A very apt description of a job on which you were expected to trudge miles checking that all staff in the prison were in post and ok and there were no problems. You were also responsible that the correct numbers of inmates were present in the various workshops and to organise the statutory exercise periods.

The job began the following day starting with ensuring that enough staff were available to man the route to the prisoners places of work. The normal staffing was 10 I was left with 5, 3 of which were plain clothes. I called control to enquire if any more staff were available – bearing in mind that this was the aftermath of a riot and tension was still running high. A voice broke in saying, "I'm on my way to the Kardomah"(the staff tearoom). The voice didn't take the regulars long to recognise – It was the Chief officer. Doors burst open from all over and in no time at all it was overflowing with staff and the tearoom was decidedly empty. I wonder why?

Then came a very slow procession of prisoners who really dragged their heels getting into work. An hour later and they were still coming.

At lunchtime I took my time after their performance to get them back into their wings.

After lunch an outside trustee who I knew from my Birmingham days approached me. "They didn't like that Gaffer and some dinners were cold".

I told him to tell them that if they got to work in reasonable time I would ensure that they would be back into their wings for meals twice as fast.

They - to my relief – responded and I kept my word. The system worked well and I didn't seem to have any problem afterwards, at least in that particular area.

Being in civilian clothes had its disadvantages especially with the prisoner's canine population. Dogs only recognised uniforms and unbeknown to me one was loose on the yard. I heard a loud yell and fortunately had access to a workshops iron gate. I slammed and locked the door only seconds before the huge alsatian arrived putting two paws on the bars of the gate and displaying a non too pleasant set of teeth. This was one time I was thankful to have been safely behind bars.

One thing I could not tolerate was of people who took advantage of seniority and tried to take it out of other staff. After all we were a team and should all work together. As a young officer it didn't happen to me but as I climbed the grades it happened twice. One of these times was whilst I was at Gartree.

In the course of my duties I had to check on the "Stand By" team who were in a room in case trouble erupted. They had certain relief duties to perform and were under the charge of a member of Gartree staff. As I entered the room, this man looked up "What do you want" he enquired but before I was given the opportunity to reply he returned to his card school and after making his contribution returned to me. He reeled off a list of instructions to me ordering me to relieve the kitchen – the chapel and some visits. Then winking to his colleagues saying that they were busy. I saw red and suggested that the best thing that he could do was to do the jobs, which he had allocated to me. I then introduced myself, as the P.O. in charge and he reluctantly complied.

I am a great believer in working with and not against staff. You tend to get much more out of them by enlisting their support.

The other incident occurred when we were returning a particularly violent young man to safer confines again in civilian clothes. The officer I was with was seniority conscious and started issuing orders. This was fine until he suggested that I became handcuffed to the prisoner. I said "No, I think you have got that wrong" and reversed the decision that after I introduced myself. It was a silent journey and I don't think that the prisoner even dare to play up after sizing up the gloomy look on his escorts face!

I feel that the situation was calmed by sheer weight of numbers and only the bravest or most foolish prisoner would dare to kick the system. There was rarely a day when some prisoner wasn't shipped out for misbehaviour. There were some very nasty characters contained in there and all staff needed constant back up because often a nasty situation arose without warning.

If we had any spare time, which was rare, we would spend it in a public house in Market Harborough. A Longsdale belt holder ran this pub and attracted quite a number of tasty characters some of whom had obviously spent time as our guests. They were well aware of who we were but were absolutely great. We joined their darts and dominoes teams and in exchange they gave us some excellent home cooked food. When you are away from home hospitality such as they afforded us was most welcomed.

The prison establishment always appeared to me as a powder keg just waiting to explode. An oppressive atmosphere loomed and one always felt a sense of unease.

My opinion is that too many inexperienced staff were given postings to this type of establishment directly out of training and were unaware of the implications and hidden dangers. The experience was unfortunately on the other foot the prisoners were the ones who were streetwise knowing their rights completely bearing in mind that they had all day to pit their wits against staff. Over my years of experience I found that if you start a regime fairly strictly you can always relax certain parts but if you try to tighten up a relaxed regime then you can have problems.

I think that the balance should be re-dressed and staff encouraged to volunteer for postings to dispersal prisons after having served 12 months in a local prison first.

I felt guilty earning the same salary in an open prison as a colleague of the same rank at a place like Gartree, Long Lartin or Parkhurst who are continually facing constant danger. I am not saying that no danger exists in open conditions but the odds of attack are far greater in a top security jail.

Salaries for work in these prisons should be equated according to risk or danger.

Just as we had got the system up and running the panic was over and I was returned to my own establishment. I missed Gartree because in some ways it formed a challenge and gave one a sense of achievement.

I was not long back at Onley when I was invited to attend a promotion board for the rank of Principal Officer.

I attended and after being asked many questions some of which were hypothetical and attempts being made to put you on the spot or to change your mind I returned. I felt more confident on this one and for once I was right I was placed on the list to await promotion in the meantime it was decided by management that I would cover many of the higher grades absences i.e. annual leave, sickness. I found this provided excellent grounding.

It was not without its problems. Staff and inmates alike were somewhat suspicious of new faces because they had been used to their own I/C's system. I did not attempt to enforce change. Gradually the boys and staff began to accept me and just as I was getting more conversant with the different systems I was called up and offered a posting on promotion to Sudbury in Derbyshire.

Before accepting I was allowed to pre-visit the establishment, meet the staff hear what the job entails and look at properties. See if they like you and most importantly if you are happy with the posting.

The area was beautiful and the job seemed fine so I accepted.

Like a housing chain the Governor of your old establishment would not let you go until getting a replacement Senior Officer. The Officer promoted would not be allowed to move until a replacement officer had been provided – this could take ages. Anyhow a few strings were pulled and away I went.

Phoenix House

I explained that the Phoenix Plaque was competed by the boys for the best overall weekly performance.

Another Phoenix featured not in competition but in challenge. This referred to a drug withdrawal unit in London started off by two. New Yorkers who I had the privilege of meeting when they came to Onley to interview a boy prior to accepting him on a rehabilitation course.

The two had been right through the problem having both apparently been addicts of drug abuse.

Their methods were unconventional to say the least. As we entered the room they were using for the interview they totally ignored us. Eventually the man beckoned me to sit down but blanked off the boy who started to sit down. "Who told you to sit" enquired the man. The boy was taken off balance completely and then ignoring him. Suddenly and without warning the women yelled at the boy "Why the f*** should we take you?" Her nose was about an inch from the lads. He didn't flinch but just calmly explained that the reason was that he wished to kick the habit and the clinic seemed the best way. The girl flickered a smile, remarking that the answer provided a good enough reason.

After this the interview took on a more relaxed style. The couple both introduced themselves and talked to the boy at length and after allowed his return asked me to remain.

During this they explained how the system would work. Upon arrival their heads were shaved as they were not to be allowed out for the first month and by doing this they were less likely to wish to go out. After this they were put under the charge of a more senior boy.

Each member as part of the programme was allocated work. Usually a soul destroying type of job such as scrubbing or something similar. As they progressed through the course the jobs became more interesting and they took on more responsibility perhaps office or stores work then suddenly and for no given reason they were knocked back down to scrubbing floors and had to work their way back up. If they succeeded they would stay in the better job.

The idea of this was to build up their strength of character to enable them to withstand any pressures the course would bring. The organisers wouldn't discuss the actual therapy involved but claimed to have a very high rate of success. Whatever way they employed I did not envy the lad. I was invited to visit whilst the course was taking place but couldn't make it.

As for the couple running the course there are none more experienced than those who have actually passed along the same road and during the initial stage a very favourable article was included in the Guardian newspaper, explaining the sheer hell experienced by this husband and wife team to cure the addiction.

The sad facts are that it kills. I recall one boy who used to spend a lot of time talking to me. I desperately tried to warn him against the habit and he was on some form of medication.

I used to say "You know what will happen if you don't kick this habit" He replied "Yes, I will be dead".

Not very long after his release he was back on the habit despite our warnings and true to his word he died.

An arrogant character but still had a lot of living to do at nineteen.

SUDBURY

taking the scenic route into Derbyshire – I hate motorways! They're ok for fast travel but not for me – I prefer to take in the fabulous view of the countryside, which was going to be our future home.

The promotion made me want to go but suddenly I became home sick. Had I made the right decision? After all I had left behind my wife and a baby daughter. Was promotion all that important. I now know the answer but never the less continued on my way.

Upon arrival I presented myself at Sudbury prison gate, where I received a much more friendly welcome than I had previously experienced from encounters with other gatekeepers.

I was escorted to the administration block and introduced to my new boss. As it happened he was a person I knew quite well from my days at Gartree. Again the welcome was vastly different from those of the past.

Whilst I stood talking I felt a numbness coming into my right elbow. It couldn't be? Or could it? Looking around I saw the beaming smile and the ruddy face of an old colleague from my Birmingham days. This man a jovial stocky ex brewers drayman, had the strength of a lion and had perfected a grip using his thumb and forefinger which, when applied had the similar effect of a vice being tightened resulting in a numbness which lasted for ages.

He was salt of the earth. Not many left, more's the pity. When I was at Birmingham he guided me through the Winson Green's maze, and fortunately he was here to do it again. Although I vowed not for him to apply the fateful grip – not if I could help it. I must admit he caught me a few times off guard and I paid the ultimate penalty.

As the time came nearer for him to retire we were all engaged in deep conversation in the orderly room – a place where the PO's and SO's congregated, he caught me unawares. Applying the grip I just carried on talking. A voice in my ear said, "AM I LOSING MY GRIP?"

133

I replied to the effect that no, and it was killing me, but I was determined not to give in. However, I paid the penalty afterwards.

The service needed people like him, because besides enjoying the practical jokes he was a very good officer.

My responsibilities were explained and we set off on a guided tour of the establishment. It housed just over 300 category 'D' inmates. Category 'D' being prisoners considered by the authorities to present the least risk to the public. This was usually a true picture, but every rule has its exceptions.

My promotion arose because Sudbury was due to take on the role of accommodating life sentence prisoners, who were nearing consideration for release, and open prison gave them the opportunity to show that they were capable of coping with this challenge.

At first, this move, as would be expected, caused the nearby villagers considerable concern and media coverage accelerated this problem. However, the villagers slowly accepted this, some becoming involved in the system forming their own lifer committees.

The prison had been converted from an old American service hospital, to the first Midlands open prison in late 1940, and was a series of dormitories housing around 35 inmates in each dorm. During heavy storms, some dormitories were liable to flood, several times I saw inmates and staff with trousers rolled up to their knees, wading through water in an effort to clear up. At times like this it was amazing how staff and inmates would work together. A small portion was converted to wash and toilet facilities and an even smaller section provided double rooms allocated in seniority order. In this area we emphasised that we did not intend that lifers would get any priority over any other prisoner. Eventually we wouldn't be able to avoid this because of the length of their sentences, but at this stage we didn't want them getting the feeling that they were something special.

Bed spaces were each individuals personal responsibility, all blankets and sheets being neatly boxed – the bed spaces have now been converted into separate rooms, which not only give individuals privacy and cutting down on dorm thefts, but also alleviates the problem of room allocation.

As we continued our tour, one thing I couldn't get used to. Up until now all the prisons I had served in or visited had secure doors which were always unlocked and re-locked when you moved from place to place, but here there was nothing like this – NO LOCKS anywhere.

The area was huge with a large pond dominating the East side. My guide explained that it was used by inmates for fishing. I laughed, thinking that this was another phase of a weird sense of humour, my colleague said that he wasn't joking. He wasn't! A prisoner had to apply to join the fishing club and must be in possession of one vital item of equipment, namely a discorger.

The main objective of the fisherman was to land a huge fish, a tench I think, which was supposed to be lurking around the area. To my knowledge, at my time of retirement, no one had succeeded.

Continuing the tour we headed towards the industrial complex, comprising a variety of manufacturing workshops producing items of furniture, all types of prison footwear, including boots, shoes and slippers – the latter having bright yellow piping around the edges. I still have a penholder made in this material which wears and wears. The shoes were punched with a special ring making them identifiable should they reach the open market, which they sometimes did, fetching good prices. Sometimes prisoners in these workshops made their own prototypes, with a hollow swivel heel to secrete illegal items in.

I was shown the laundry, which besides washing for the prison, catered for other prisons, some hospitals and military establishments. Later a full dry cleaning plant was installed.

Staff and inmate labour carried out all maintenance. Most skilled tradesmen serving sentences were used to advantage. We even had our own welding shop.

The vast area was maintained by the Garden department to a very high standard. This department had achieved top awards in national gardening competitions and on occasions supplied all the colourful baskets for the nearby market town of Uttoxeter.

Afterwards, I was introduced to members of the prisons education staff – a dedicated section and very popular with the inmates. They offered a wide range of subjects, from very basics, ie: teaching reading and writing – it was surprising that even in this day and age how many were unable to read and write. At the other end of the scale they prepared some inmates for sitting for degrees. A popular half way house was business studies, also computers.

Evening studies and leisure activities were on offer, the most popular being art and model making. Several Vocational Training Standard classes provided certificates in bricklaying, painting and decorating and motor mechanics. Standards would make most D.I.Y. men very envious indeed. All of these courses were led by highly professional trainers and their pass rate spoke volumes.

Continuing our tour I was shown the staff bachelor quarters, this was to be my temporary home for quite a while. Not very impressive, old and slowly eroding, I felt that probably the prisoners had a better deal. Suddenly my pang for home comforts returned. I supposed the only consolation was that the officers club and mess was very close to hand and at least I could drown my sorrows. the club also presented an ideal opportunity for meeting my future colleagues socially.

After a good nights sleep I reported for my first day and was shown the wing which I was to take charge of, and also introduced to my second in command, a long served senior officer with a wide range of experience, of both open and closed prison management. He was a very nice man, but one who had been passed by for promotion. I had the distinct feeling that at this stage he resented a somewhat younger, less wise man taking over, but this was how it was and nothing would change it. As often is the case we were to get on extremely well.

After my induction he would refer all of the prisoners queries to me, saying to them, "You had better see the PO, he will decide." Initially I accepted these referrals, but afterwards decided that many of the requests were well within his capabilities to deal with, so I used to re-refer them to him saying, "I'm sure you don't need me to make a decision on something you are more than able to act on." The cat and mouse game continued for a short while longer and then suddenly it ceased. I am sure he got the message.

The day began with Prisoners' applications to the Governor. Like the SO many could be dealt with at my level. The idea being that the PO would sift through and save the Governor time.

Applications would include letters for special purposes ie: to police, probation, employer, or other courts to have outstanding fines taken into consideration whilst in custody. Most of these letters were on prison headed letter sheets, but there was one exception, this was a letter to a child in hospital for which no headings were on the letter sheet.

136

Other applications were to have authorised items sent in, ie: sportswear, fishing equipment (including discorger), musical instruments, radios or cassette players. No item with electrical connections was allowed for obvious reasons and shavers could only be battery operated. Radios had to have earpieces because in an open dormitory not everyone's choice of programme suited the others and situations such as these could easily flare up and cause trouble.

The other applications involved authorising prisoners to spend or send out private cash, this mainly related to long term prisoners who often sent money to their relatives.

Some came for advice or to pass on information. Each day brought something different, making the job so very interesting. The down side was that you were fully responsible for your own decisions right or wrong and you took both the brickbats or accolades as the case may be.

Some religions offered exotic food on feast days, and some of the smart alec's attempted to change religion to obtain the full benefits.

This day a young man entered my office applying to change from Moslem to Jew. Seeing this as a complete mickey take I picked up the phone speaking to the medical centre and related this man's request. He said he would come over because a circumcision would be required. I relayed this information to the prisoner who was already disappearing through the door saying, "forget it boss, I've changed my mind." Didn't see much more of him throughout his sentence. This was one time when I called his bluff and succeeded, however, this was not always the case. Often it misfired against us.

Following applications we would adjourn to the Orderly Room for a cup of tea and a chat. This was the place where PO's and SO's convened for a chat, perhaps about the days plans or entirely different subjects such as topical events or sport.

An Error I'm Glad I Didn't Make

As I have said before, that to enable them survive, staff seemed to develop a weird sense of humour and on this particular occasions, two senior officers were continually having friendly digs at each other by playing practical jokes. This time one decided to empty the contents of an ashtray into the others cap, not in hindsight a very hygienic thing to do, but I did say staff had a very odd sense of humour. There were smiles all round the orderly room, people imagining the reaction when the wearer came to put his hat on. However, the joke misfired, especially on the joker because the hat he had used was not the one he intended it to be, instead the owner was the brewers' drayman. A change of face and a quick departure was made by the joker because of the possible repercussions.

We waited in anticipation of the owners reaction, but there wasn't any, the owner simply emptied the cap into a nearby bin, dusted it off, made some adverse comment and departed. I am confident that he got his revenge later, plus he did not give us the satisfaction of witnessing it. As for the joker, he was conspicuous by his absence, who knows? perhaps his elbow was paralysed. Despite the fact the joke was not in the best of taste, everyone in the orderly room departed that evening wearing a smile, especially at the way the joke rebounded and of the perpetrators rapid change of direction. It certainly dispelled the days distresses, except for one person.

The tea room was run by a prisoner trustee and throughout my time at Sudbury, have met Solicitors, Estate Agents, Police Officers, our own kind and a variety of businessmen, all very interesting conversationalists and not one to my knowledge professed being innocent. Sometimes I used to think that, 'There but for the grace of God go I.'

Prisoners were beginning to congregate on the parade square for the morning work parade, despite the fact that open prison regimes were more free and easy than closed ones, the discipline at least at this time was stricter. It does not happen now more's the pity – in my opinion lowering of standards is not a good thing when you are effecting control of groups of men, in whatever walk of life. To relax rules is relatively easy, but to try to tighten up is when trouble occurs.

Getting back to the work parade, the men formed up with their respective parties and under their party officers were marched off when the prison roll had been checked.

Monty

On each work parade am and pm, we were accompanied by an unusual visitor. He was never late and when the inmates were on parade he would walk around carrying out his own inspection. The inmates never resented him, in fact most of them looked forward to seeing him, he was the prison cat and was aptly named Montgomery!

The office staff cared for him. One day he was not punctual, in fact he didn't turn up for parade and never turned up again. No one knew the true version, but many thought that he didn't wish to show people he was ill, so he wandered off to end his days, he was very old.

We certainly missed him because he broke the ice on many occasions just by his antics and actions. A 'Top Cat' in every sense of the word who lived up to his famous name.

The morning's applications were then entered into the prisoners' record, details being taken from the application register along with an entry of the appropriate action taken. This was extremely important, because it could form part of litigation; even years later, for example, an injury occurring in prison could become aggravated later and result in a claim for compensation; or a decision made which was contested by the prisoner to a higher authority, could result in the authority requesting to see a written recording of the decision before passing judgement.

The applications being referred to the Governor would need to be processed ready for him to hear with any complicated ones being discussed with him beforehand.

Typical applications he would deal with could be for parole to visit a sick or dying relative, a complaint against staff, conditions and food or home leave. He or she would rapidly single out the time wasters or malingerers. The decisions were not always agreeable to us, but his or her decision was final.

Later I was given the authority to make such decisions, and I am certain that some of mine made my staff throw their arms up in horror. An example of this would be when a prisoner well known to me applied for leave to marry. I decided to take a chance, despite the fact that he had a colourful past to say the least, and allowed him one days parole threatening him with all sorts of horrible things should he let me down.

"Don't worry Mr P, I won't, I'll be back." He was, even carrying a piece of wedding cake for me.

After processing the applications the next job was to inspect some of the living quarters. Normally these were very tidy because we could swoop on any of the dormitories at any time.

The dormitories were laid out similar to any army barrack room with sheets and blankets neatly boxed. The idea of this was to ensure that each man opened and aired his bedding daily. Goodness knows what state they would be in with some if this had not been enforced.

One individual never slept on his bed, always under it. he was one of the many eccentrics I encountered. His reputation was similar when he was outside. he is reputed on one occasion to have climbed the wall of his local prison on Christmas Day dressed as Father Christmas, complete with sack, throwing tobacco to the very willing recipients. Another time, securing himself to a tree, aiming at attracting the authorities attention and yet another by paying a hefty fine in the lowest denomination possible.

Throughout his sentence he was no trouble whatsoever, being a workaholic he was allocated to our farm party where someone tampered with his tobacco tin. His method of retaliation, was that he announced to a full party in the mess room, that he had mixed his tobacco with some concoction from the wild which, would not kill the thief, but render then unconscious for a considerable time. Needless to say no one touched his tobacco ever again.

On the day of his release, nearly the entire population congregated to bid him farewell, amidst cheers he emerged wearing full evening dress.

The inspection complete we returned to deal with the call-ups, this being incoming mail of an official nature. Examples would be unpaid fines imposed before a prisoner was sentenced; these were known as lodged warrants and provided imprisonment in lieu of non-payment. The prisoner would have notified the Courts that he was in custody and often extra weeks of imprisonment would be imposed whilst he was in custody. Very often they would run alongside the sentence being served, so that the release date would be unaffected and the debt wiped out. This in my opinion is not why fines are imposed, but that's only my opinion. The longest term of extra imprisonment I have seen imposed by this manner added up to twelve months, and the sight of the recipients face was a sight to behold.

Other matters being dealt with under the call-up system would relate to replies concerning employment, resettlement and possibly future court appearances. Again, all of these required to be meticulously recorded in case of future repercussions.

By now queues were forming for lunch. As with every routine it was the prisoner's responsibility to attend. Much of the discipline was self-imposed. In my early days even if a prisoner had been placed on report for mis-conduct, the onus was on this person to attend for a medical and report for adjudication at the given times except offences of personal violence or obviously absconders. Eventually the system changed to the one I had been used to which is much less embarrassing should things go wrong.

After lunch the afternoons were reasonably quiet except for reception days, because it was our job to interview all arrivals and write up a brief induction report on each individual. During these interviews we would assess any outstanding problems, the type of person, their potential training requirements and risk factor, and to explain our expectations of the person.

Phrases such as, 'This man needs to be watched' or, 'I don't think he is ideally suited for this type of regime' covered a multitude of sins. If for example the man serves his sentence without problems, then the entry was never looked at, but if the person ran away or caused any other trouble the comments were seen as being correct predictions. In my early days of joining the service I was given very good advice amongst which was, 'Always leave a back door to get out of'. These turned out to be excellent words of wisdom.

In addition to induction days the afternoons were ideal for interviews and review boards.

I enjoyed parole interviews and interviewing staff for annual assessments. I certainly learnt much, the secret being to just listen and throw in the odd question here and there when needed.

Had I have been criminally minded I discovered various methods by which prisoners operated, for example, a burglar will target a specific area during the winter months observing at which houses the lights came on. They would carry this out for a week or so, and if the light did not come on during that time then it would be safe to assume that the occupants were at work. Once this did not work out – he targeted the area and the lights did not come on for two weeks in this bungalow, so he and his son decided to force an entry. they were pleased that no dogs were around or no alarms, but feeling somewhat uneasy, stole a video and one or two small items and decided to call it a day. Making their way out they were confronted by a number of police officers and after arrest discovered that the occupant was none other than the Chief Officer of Police. "Not one of my best days boss," to which I would tend to agree.

Others told me how they stole to order and carried out the theft by distraction, using an 'old banger' to make their get away, the car being expendable, they could either abandon or sell to a dealer for a few pounds.

One of the ingredients for parole eligibility was that the offender showed genuine remorse, which did not always happen. I recall one who committed a very violent form of attack; he showed no remorse at all. Needless to say he did not receive parole but did so later. When released he must have felt remorse because shortly afterwards he took his own life.

Yet another, a venison poacher, who was fully equipped for the job with a refrigerated van, was in the act when he saw two, what he thought were game keepers – his intention was to fire two shots over their heads and run. He says he fired with this high velocity weapon well above their heads and attempted to make his getaway, but being blocked by police, surrendered. What he didn't bargain for was that both would be gamekeepers turned out to be police officers.

Obviously the charge was more severe, and what could have been poaching and a nine-month sentence, finished dup as discharging a loaded firearm with intent to endanger life and the sentence was NINE YEARS. Such is life! His words, not mine. Finally a discipline officer in a 'Hells Angel" chapter, went too heavy-handed resulting in a death; he received a long sentence.

He turned to Buddhism and explained the following in extremely graphical detail, also the working of Hells Angel chapters. He attained a master's degree during his sentence. An extremely interesting character to talk to.

These interviews were taken very seriously, they were deep seated and it was very important to be completely sure of the facts. To recommend whether a person goes free or not means a lot, not only to the person but also to society, to which we owe a debt, and finally to oneself and ones own conscience. An example of this happened to me. Prior to the release of a life sentence prisoner, a review takes place based on a series of reports, one of which was our responsibility. A model prisoner was coming up for review. He had behaved impeccably; his work record was good, he responded well, also showing remorse for his crime – a one off affair, committed on foreign shores.

I reported truthfully on how I had seen him making no positive recommendation either way. Obviously the Home Secretary made the final decision after consultation with the trial judge. He was released and not long afterwards committed a particularly nasty murder. I felt in some part responsible for this, and it took a considerable while for the scars to heal despite personal re-assurances from a prison department representative.

Reports were very important, and I for one took careful consideration about what I was going to say. One report we were responsible for and one which could make or break a person was the annual staff report. This went a long ways towards determining a person's future. constructive criticism was not always received favourably because the majority of us do not like to be criticised.

I have long been against written reports, feeling that a board of say three, should conduct a review, because a biased person could ruin someone's future prospects. I am speaking from my own experience. Prior to receiving this adverse report I always received excellent ones, until being accused of taking a form of action during an industrial dispute, on a day which I was at home on my day off. I was cleared of this accusation, but am confident that the stigma remained, because I was rejected on successive promotion boards. I feel that had a board decided my fate then I would have been able to put my points over. Maybe I would still have been rejected, but would have at least had a chance. Still, it's all water under the bridge now because I retired long ago.

Evening Duties

The orderly officer during the evening was a PO assisted by an SO and when these two got together many a battle was fought, many a tale spun, and many a coffee was drunk.

This was a time when after a roll check the prisoners were allowed to pursue their leisure activities. The activities varied, some enjoying physical, such as team sports, weight lifting, indoor football or walking round and round the dormitory block, and others less physical such as model making, attending evening classes, watching T.V. and laying on their beds listening to their radios.

The prison also had its own aviary, breeding every conceivable bird, budgerigars were a speciality, so much so, that when our daughter was young, we gave her one for her birthday. One that was hand picked and whom I had monitored from the day it was hatched. It started out such a nervous little chap, but soon because a very definite member of the family. His ability to talk endlessly and the antics he got up to gave us lots of amusement. Our daughter named him Guy, from magazines called 'My Guy' and 'Oh Boy'. Unfortunately Guy passed away in 1996 at the grand old age of ten, he is one that truly could be called a real 'jail bird'.

Hobbies presented a change in my experience of previous security establishments, because the prisoners in open conditions were allowed a kit of one Stanley knife, one screwdriver, one small pin hammer and a ruler. This took me a long while to accept, but the argument in favour made sense. In an open prison, access could be gained to all sorts of objects that could have been much more dangerous, so why the fuss about a hobby kit – this gradually began to make sense to me and I suppose to some extent I accepted it. As the Governor put it, "You will eventually come round to our way of thinking," and as time passed I think I did.

The other activities, which attracted a certain group of prisoners were illegal ones, and there were plenty of these taking place. Amongst these was an operation known as 'parcel running'. the object was for a runner to venture out of bounds to the perimeter wire fence, and sometimes beyond to rendezvous with an outside supplier. he would collect a parcel of forbidden items and to deliver it to the person inside, for either his own use or to sell at a vast profit – items usually were tobacco or spirits. The runners were paid only a pittance and quite often when they were seen in training it was to train to be able to sprint from the fence to the sanctuary of the dormitories without being discovered. Usually this was financed by the richer element of the population, using the reckless or the hard up to do their donkey work for them, plus the fact that if caught the runner would be expected to take the blame and the consequences.

Sometimes these parcels were used to pay off debts. Much information was provided by other prisoners relating to parcels coming in, probably through jealously and as much as I despised informants they were very necessary. Of course sometimes the information received was false, and often the aim was to divert attention away from a specific area because that was somewhere, where either an abscond or parcel run was planned.

I remember once acting on information received, posting a senior officer in an adjacent field. It was a Saturday and all the company he had were inquisitive cows, to cap it all it rained and nothing what so ever happened. He was far from being pleased; saying that this would be the last time I would get him doing this. It wasn't however, because both he and I kept observations on a bitterly cold Sunday evening, with I don't know how many degrees of frost, collars high and for nothing. Often this is the way and at the most unexpected time you are successful.

Going off duty after an evening patrol, a group of us walked past the outer doors of the dormitories, loudly expressing how much we were going to enjoy the first pint. Not to aggravate the population – or may be just a bit, but mainly to appear to be going home – the truth of the matter was that following yet another tip off we were going to keep observations. Quickly we spread out across the area and it wasn't long after that by the courtesy of a street light we saw a figure climb the other fence, which wasn't very high, and jump into the grounds and vanish into the darkness. It was a question of where he was likely to appear because it was much too dark to identify him. Suddenly this figure rushed out of the shadows heading straight for me. I saw that he was armed with a cosh type weapon. With not much time to think I called "Stop! Or I'll send the dog." Luckily for me he stopped, threw his weapon down and surrendered a very large parcel of tobacco, spirits and even hot chicken rolls. By this time my colleagues had joined me and as they walked him away he started making some derogatory remarks to me after realising that there weren't any dogs in open prisons.

A long time after this he laughed about the incident, but certainly not at this time. It was about a year later, and even then he tried his hand at smuggling a parcel of jeans to outside contacts. No wonder after he was caught bang to rights that he earned the nickname of 'Road Runner'.

It would be wrong of me to try to create the impression that people trafficking were only bringing supplies into the prison – this was not the case at all because items of prison clothing commanded high prices in open markets, particularly prison shirts. Whilst on the subject of shirts. One day I was sitting in my office with the door open. Hearing a noise I went to investigate. The noise was coming from the toilet area, upon entering I was confronted by a prisoner. "I'm glad I've seen you Mr P, I've just found these," handing me a parcel containing these new shirts. "I think someone's trying to nick them." That was at least true – he was! He worked in the stores, he admitted to this later. Had he got away with it, it wouldn't have been a bad days work, £25 each times 12, equals 3300. As it was it cost him instead loss of remission.

Another occasion this man was hiding somewhere in the undergrowth, waiting his chance to bring a parcel in. It was very dark, a voice said, "Come on quick, the screws have gone. It's clear in A dorm." he made a dash for it, running straight into the welcoming arms of officers. The person giving him clearance was in fact a member of staff. This was a deterrent for the others and a sickener for him.

I have mentioned decoys, well the Orderly Room roof had been subject to a number of attacks by an anonymous stone thrower, quite disturbing it was too. We had a very good idea of the culprit but no proof. After talking it over we decided to mount observations on the other side, just in case, and it paid off, because after we had caught the runner the mysterious stone throwing episode ceased. I wonder why?

We were not always on the winning side, once I chased a figure that disappeared into a dormitory. Being out of breath – not as young as I used to be – I sat on a bed in the dorm, after recovering continued on my way. We did not find the parcel runner. Two days later one of my informants told me that the bed on which I sat had the parcel under it. Still you cannot possibly win them all.

Inspection days were Sundays of the Governor and Wednesdays for the Chief Officer accompanied by his PO's. The standards were high, and any one falling below expectations would be in trouble.

Many humorous incidents occurred, but one of my favourites was during the governors inspection. His inspection would take place around ten in the morning, and being a Sunday the remainder of the day was their own provided of course, that everything was up to the required standard. As he wandered around inspecting he would engage the occupants in conversation. If a man had a model, say a jewellery box, he would ask the prisoner if the model had a musical movement – these they could purchase from the hobbies officer – if it had he would ask them to play it.

He would repeat this to all with models, probably seventy-five per cent and by the time he had completed, there would be the most horrible cacophony of sound emerging, that the governor would walk out quietly chuckling to himself. This wasn't a game, because he didn't miss a trick, and he would spot anything out of place in an instant, the slightest speck of dust he would spot. As he put it, "After the inspection, it's their time, so it's up to them what they do with it."

He was a pilot during the war earning the DFC, and an exceptionally shrewd man who commanded much respect from his staff. His decisions sometimes were unorthodox, but certainly worked. it was rumoured that whilst at a training prison he was faced with a 'sit down' by prisoners on the sports field. Despite all his efforts to clear the field they remained, refusing to move. After evening meal he returned with a tractor and driver. As he alighted he was asked what he was doing. He is said to have replied, "Well if you are not going to use it as a sports field, I may as well plough it up and plant cabbages." To which the prisoners rapidly dispersed because the last thing they wanted was to lose their sports field.

Governors all had their own individual styles of managing. We had Governors like this one and several others I have known who belonged to the old school and believed in the hard bed, hard board system. they were extremely astute and what they didn't know about Prison Rules was not worth knowing. Others used more liberal systems, not always going down too well with the old 'die hard' officers, but never the less they seemed to work. They allowed more prisoners to go on home leave at Christmas expecting disaster to strike, nothing happened and virtually all returned on time. More out workers were found jobs in industry, farms and care homes. Those achieving these jobs got excellent comments from their employers and elderly people were getting their gardens dug and houses decorated.

I came to the conclusion that if you were honest and fair to prisoners, and despite all the relaxation in the rules, then they were highly unlikely to let you down.

Unfortunately these days the Governor has very little chance to move out of his office because he is constantly engulfed in paperwork. He or she seems more likely to have the skills of an accountant than a prison governor. The Governor used to be able to get out and about, knew all of his staff and any possible problems, and many of the inmates. Also they got to know him, now they have to delegate to junior staff and especially large prisons, some of the staff do not know, 'The Old Man'.

In my junior days wherever you went, you seemed to bump into the Governor. I recall once, two of us were supervising the erection of a new gymnasium,. The builders had only completed the shell and it was a typical winter's day with the wind howling around us. As no contractor could get in for a least two hours, we decided to toss up to see who would go to the officers' mess next to us for a cup of tea. I won, but wished I hadn't, because no sooner had I ordered a drink and contemplated a bacon sandwich, the door burst open and in walks the Chief Officer, the Governor and accompanied by another man. Who, to my detriment I was to discover was a prison commissioner on his annual tour of inspection.

The Chief not at all pleased, beckoned me outside not giving me a chance to explain, gave me the biggest rollicking I have ever had. He didn't use the same expletive twice, a definite master of the english language or should I say, Anglo-Saxon. My mate watching from the sidelines was doubled up with laughter. An ex R.S.M. himself, I am sure he had dished out his fair share of the same in the past saw it as amusing.

The Chief long since passed on was a nasty ferocious little man, left me with a lasting impression making me determined never to treat staff in this manner should I reach any dizzy heights in the rank structure, and I don't think I ever did.

I remember being late one day. I had struggled the eleven miles in dense fog. I think I was a quarter of an hour adrift, but no thanks, just another lecture for not getting up earlier. The same Chief, a devout Roman Catholic, was well known for having officers removed from their supervisory duties because they were not of the Roman Catholic faith. I was one removed from this job. he would simply press the alarm bell, await the arrival of the heavy mob and replace us with staff he knew to be Roman Catholic.

Also, whilst at prayer he would place his hands together, but split his fingers slightly, watching for any of the congregation who were talking. Not only would they receive a tongue lashing from him, but also, incur the wrath of the priest as well. I thought, what strange people.

During roll checks, which were a frequent part of each day's routine, it became the prisoners personal responsibility to attend. Absences were only allowed if they had been authorised by staff.

Each dormitory was checked by an officer and each man counted. The numbers were reported to the orderly officer and checked against the master roll board, if the numbers given agreed, then the prison population would be allowed to return to normal activities, be it leisure or work, depending on the time of day. If however, they did not agree, then a re-check would take place. It was during these times that we would discover absconds, but before this a thorough search of the area including all known hiding places would be carried out. At this stage we would not discount the fact that someone could have been assaulted, taken ill or even died. All three have happened, but invariably the missing individuals had absconded.

We would then activate an abscond routine, which involved a pre-arranged plan between the police, and us both the inner and outer perimeter would be scoured.

During an abscond, two of us were carrying out a search of the area, surrounding the prison as was the normal routine. It was late summer, as we were walking around the edge of a cornfield we spotted a figure, which appeared to be running. We called for him to stop, but he ignored our instructions, slowly disappearing. We raced round the edge of the field to head him off, I shouted for him to give himself up, where upon he swerved and fell off his cycle, it wasn't a prisoner, it was a farm labourer riding his cycle from work, returning home. He was travelling down hill, thus giving the impression that he was running and ducking down at the same time. He was scared, we felt stupid and I'm sure the absconder was laughing his socks off miles away.

Cover ups would take place in various ways, for example, a prisoner would cover for an absentee by standing in the missing prisoners bed space during a head count and quickly double to his own bed space for the count in his own dormitory, usually through an open window. This was one reason that we liked to keep the regular dormitory officers checking their own dormitories, because they knew each person and could quickly identify an impostor.

The other way to counteract this ploy would be for each officer to enter their dormitory at exactly the same time. This was the ideal method but more often than not staff availability did not allow for this to be put into operation.

Another method to cover up an abscond during the night would be by creating a model of a human frame and placing this in the absentees bed and quite often this would resemble some one asleep, accentuating the limbs, and in the dark would easily pass for someone sleeping. This was known as a dummy and usually was made with a mop and pillow, creased to resemble someone curled up in bed. Usually the discovery would not be made until the following morning. Not funny to the staff, but hilarious to other occupants of the dorm.

Why they went to these lengths I don't really know because invariably they would make their way home and this would be the first port of call for the police. Hence a quick arrest and return to more secure conditions, plus probably the loss of 80 to 100 days remission.

Often the cause of absconds would be family problems, in debt to the barons or being caught out of bounds fetching a parcel.

Whilst on the subject of roll checks. One evening, whilst Orderly Officer, I was waiting for the staff to complete checking the dormitories when suddenly I was attracted to a sight and couldn't believe my eyes. At the bottom of the corridor was a man wearing a top hat and riding a unicycle – a one-wheeled bike – I shouted to the staff to get down there, but I don't think they believed me, because they took their time and by the time they had arrived the person had vanished. I'm sure they all thought that the 'Old Fool' had at last gone made, and to be quite honest so did I, until, one day, months later when I received a phone call from a discharged prisoner to say that I had not been seeing things because one of the prison workshops assembled and packed children's cycles, one of these had been converted into a unicycle and the top hat borrowed from the prison theatre. I was extremely grateful not to be going mad.

Another time, whilst a very early morning roll check was being carried out, I was awaiting the roll to be reported when something attracted my attention to the floor. To my horror a large brown rat was sitting at my feet, not the most welcomed company at any time, especially first thing in the morning. He quickly scampered off, disappearing into a gully.

In addition to this a wide variety of wild life existed around the prison and included foxes, badgers, rabbits, pheasants and a whole range of wild geese, even a swan proudly displayed her signet.s Something I will say in favour of the prisoners, they rarely, if ever caused harm to them, in fact, they used to feed the swans who in return created an awful mess.

A part of my job was to tour the prison visiting staff and during one of these trips I called in to check the fire officer who was replenishing the fire extinguishers. Upon opening one we discovered not fire fighting liquid, but what is known in prison as hooch – fermented materials to make a potent alcoholic concoction, sometimes topped up with metal polish – if you think this sounds awful, I would invite you to taste it.

As we would never find the perpetrators of this it was disposed of. I question whether even in their minds this was a wise move. Yes, it secreted it away from staff, but what if there had been a fire!

If you can understand that once convicted, a prisoner was banned from alcohol, so to break the ban and drink what is lethal could have catastrophic results.

Christmas time was a favourite time for stockpiling illegal items, and there was no problem hiding it, in fact, I felt that sometimes a Churchill tank could be hidden in there.

Earlier I outlined the workshop complex and this was usually a place where items could be secreted inside the big machines, often in the big waste bins, and on one search we found four bottles of whiskey hidden inside boxes of black pellets used in the process of shoe making.

Once we received information that a 'blow up doll' was being loaned out – for cash – of course, and although it wasn't discovered, at least to my knowledge, but in my mind I'm sure that it existed.

Lifers

As I have said, absconds were part of the risk taken in open prisons, because of the cost cutting effect of limited security. If someone was determined to go then there wasn't much to stop him, most of them didn't advertise their intentions; however, the issue became more serious when we started taking prisoners serving life sentences. The issue was the subject of much media coverage.

It was part of the PO's job before a lifer arrived to visit his parent prison to see both the prisoner and the staff to enable us to form a picture of the character we were receiving.

This was a very important step towards freedom. if you like a chink of light at the end of the tunnel, bearing in mind that the prisoner could have been in prison for anything up to 20 years, some longer, others shorter. They had been in a single cell and were now having to face living in dormitory conditions with anything up to 35 others, most of who were serving much shorter sentences.

To start with we painted a picture of open conditions as being much stricter than in fact it actually was. This was mainly to gauge a prisoner's reaction; many did not want to be moved and would petition the Home Secretary to remain where they were. However, the reply usually was to the effect that before release could be considered they were required to complete a period in open conditions.

These visits were very useful and many things could be gained from them including the prisoners reaction and attitude, for example, one walked into the interview room, put his feet on the table and proceeded to tell us what he expected of open prison. He was most offended when I, in no uncertain terms told him what I demanded, ie: to quickly get his feet off the table and listen. I was to discover this to be an act, because when he arrived I have never met a more insecure individual.

You also got a background to his offence and the judges recommendations. His own skills and the use he could be within the prison and also most importantly, his compliance with staff and rules, ie: how often he had been on report for offences against prison discipline. Certain amounts of latitude was allowed for, because anyone serving fifteen years or more was bound to fall foul of the laws at sometime.

We would then return and submit a comprehensive report and action plan for the person's future.

During my visits to talk to lifers around the country I used to travel on one day, stay overnight and return the following day. I was responsible for finding my own accommodation and it was during one of these quests that the story I'm about to relate happened.

The visit was to Northumberland, a place I've visited before. My usual accommodation – a hotel – was full. I searched around and eventually came across a 'bed and breakfast' sign.

Knocking on the door the knock was responded to by a little old lady dressed in a long skirt, woolly hat with a scarf wrapped around her neck. I explained my predicament and in turn she invited me in and proceeded to give me a rather lengthy talk on do's and don'ts. I didn't want to stay, but being worn out I accepted. I think I was faced with 'Hobsons Choice'.

During the evening I visited the prison officers club, sitting with a couple of old colleagues. I related this rather strange encounter, explaining the location, they both sported wide grins. The evening passed with us all talking over old times. I departed, returned to the digs wondering what was in store for me. However, nothing happened and being tired quickly drifted into sleep.

I awoke next morning with a knock and morning tea, served by a big man. A busy day ahead, I washed and dressed and made my way to breakfast. I was alone, when in walks a beautiful blonde, clad in a diaphanous night-dress and little else, accompanied by a large alsation. She was very pleasant, enquiring if I had a good night and was the bed comfortable. The bed was comfortable, but I certainly wasn't, making my excuses and a rapid departure after paying.

Glad to get out and back to the prison, I related the next episode of my story to my two colleagues, again, they sported the cheshire cat grin and saying that I was puzzled as to the whereabouts of the old lady and explained to me that I was unlikely to see the old lady again, because they were both the same person. Needless to say I didn't book there again, because goodness knows what would have happened.

When the lifer arrived he would usually be allocated to the wing run by the PO who visited him and would allocate one of his staff as a case officer. Ideally selecting an officer who matched the lifer in temperament and interest. I was lucky I had a wide variety to choose from, including an ex-pro footballer who was very interested in casework. He played hard on and off the field, and was very well respected by all the lifers. Some needed a father figure and others strong-minded characters.

Each lifer was subjected to regular reviews, which were very carefully structured to meet the lifers case plan. For this, reports were submitted by any staff dealing with the lifer, ie: his employer, the gym staff, education staff, chaplain and of course his case officer who was listened to very carefully, especially if he had any particular ideas regarding future plans.

After the prisoner was seen, the board decided upon future plans. As his stay lengthened, so extra degrees of responsibility were given to him. It could be joining an outside working party or being allowed to go to away fixtures with one of the sports teams or being taken to a city for a day with his case officer, to become once again acquainted with shopping, bearing in mind that some hadn't even seen decimal currency. If they went into a china shop the officer was only too pleased to emerge without having to pay for any broken china. This was also a testing time, to see if the lifer would try to abscond, because the opportunity was there. Very few tried, of those who did they were the losers, because they would be returned to closed conditions and it could be anything up to 4 years before they were able to return to an open prison.

When a lifer settled into a dormitory it seemed to have a stabilising effect on the remainder of occupants, especially the young, would-be tearaways.

We tried to treat them as we would any other prisoner, giving them nothing more or less than their legal entitlements, this worked to a degree, but not completely, for example, the lifer was allowed readjustment visits, his length of stay would usually ensure that he was allocated a room, he was always aware of his progress or lack of, as the case may be, whereas, at this stage a prisoner with a definitive sentence did not get any of these, and could not guarantee they would get a room. This initially caused quite a few bones of contention from the others who saw this as favouritism.

Jogging was a favourite pastime of the lifers, with one of the staff taking them during his lunch break. They thought the world of him. I often asked them why they chose this form of sport during my interviews, and with very few exceptions the answer was that it gave them the time to think about their past, without being interrupted.

Much of their time was spent studying and a large number finished up securing degrees, and were rewarded upon release with good jobs.

Another was an excellent guitarist and broadcasted several times on local radio. One, an excellent potter, created his own style of pottery. On his release he set-up his own business in the West Country. In fact he made me a mug of enormous proportions, which my prisoner orderly would only ever half fill saying, "Anymore in there and you'll drown, Guv."

Sometimes during a lifer board, we would put a man to the test to see his reaction by criticising something and watching for their response. Occasionally, they would become quite aggressive, even getting close to blows. After they had calmed down we would explain that it was not only essential, but vital that they kept cool, because should they be fortunate enough to get a job when released if they reacted like they had just done to a manager or supervisor then they would rapidly be out of work and could be returned to prison because a life sentenced prisoner is on licence for the entire time he or she lives.

If we thought it necessary we could refer prisoners to a visiting psychiatrist and part of the release plan was that eventually they would be interviewed by a psychiatrist. An understanding of his wrongdoing and a sense of remorse was essential before a lifer was considered for release.

Over the years I have received numerous letters from lifers to let me know how they have progressed, ie: marrying and work, plus how they have seen the outside world. I appreciated these letters and have always kept them, sometimes re-reading them.

One lad, who I knew previously from Borstal, since committed murder and served his time, wrote to me saying he had married and was enjoying family life. He clearly comes to mind because, during his interview I was somewhat disturbed to discover that his interest was nuclear weaponry. I tackled him on this and his reply was quite interesting. He said that the day after he had received his sentence of life imprisonment he was in Wormwood Scrubs sitting, waiting to be interviewed, he was very down in the dumps. Sitting opposite him was an old lifer shortly due for release. "Go over there and pick up a book" he said, pointing to a table displaying magazines. "Now open it at any page." This he did, "Whatever the subject, study it throughout your sentence. You will learn much and time will pass." The subject he opened the book at was nuclear warfare. Thank goodness that the business he set-up in was Painter and Decorator!

Naturally if a prisoner absconded the villagers were concerned but even more so with the lifers. A lifer liaison committee was set-up, comprising representatives from neighbouring villages, police and prison. Discussing any apparent problems and early warning systems should a lifer abscond, although they didn't need much warning, because the area was swarming with police and press. The latter I found to be leaping at the opportunity of publishing anything sensational, which happened in prison. Some of the publicity we could have done without, especially in the early stages. Politicians were often involved, rightly so, especially when something went wrong.

Should a lifer escape and frighten the occupants of the village, as one did, then the questions would come thick and fast – demands such as why did such a man come to open conditions, with such a background? The answer was simple, we didn't make the decisions as to whether they should come or not, all we did was explain the system and paint a pen picture of the person. The final decision rested at ministerial level.

Many lifers turned to religion, at one stage all the servers, the altar boy, most of the choir and the chapel orderly were all lifers. All denominations were catered for and either visiting or regular clergy were on hand to cater for their own followers' needs.

As with all things in prison the element of manipulators would try to make the system work to their advantage. Certain faiths provided food on feast days. The manipulators would attempt to change their religion to gain this advantage, but unfortunately permission had to be obtained from the the minister to whose faith they belonged and the minister of the religion they wished to join. Often one of these ministers would see through the ploy and block the change, genuine applicants would however, be dealt with on their own merits.

One popular belief amongst the lifers was the Buddhist way of living. Christian fellowship groups were extremely popular and usually were held on Friday evenings. They attracted a wide range of speakers, including sports personalities, traveller and missionaries, but the most popular were the musical groups. The inmates were usually well behaved, but like everywhere there was always the odd idiot.

A girl singer had just completed her song and amidst the applause this one shouted, "Get em off", the girl as quick as a flash replied, "I'm sorry, I can't because I haven't got any on," much to the delight of the remainder of the audience and the total embarrassment of the idiot.

The chapel, as many are, was open at all times, even in the chaplain's absence, and it wasn't always used as intended. The more shady types used it as a meeting point to plan parcel runs or share out the spoils. Bookies and barons also converged, I am sure that some of the devout believers had ulterior motives and were more out to line their own pockets rather than to worship.

Observing these activities was not easy because lookouts were used. Darker nights were much easier because it was much harder for them to spot us.

With the change of the social pattern, drugs in prison being a real problem, the most regularly used being cannabis in its various guises.

The presence of drugs constantly created a source of anxiety and a big danger in prisons. Demand was high, prices were high and the users were high. Suppliers were making much money and lack of supplies caused tension. Staff needed to continually monitor by regular searches and gathering of intelligence information.

In the following paragraphs I have tried to explain some of the ingenious methods which have been tried by suppliers to smuggle the stuff in.

The smell of cannabis could easily be detected – it smells like burning grass, but discovering who were the users was a much bigger problem. To me it was like when someone lights a smelly bonfire, you are aware of its presences, but finding its source is an entirely different matter. Just imagine the task in an open dormitory situation. Ten dorms and the smell begins to drift into the corridor, staff may be lucky enough to detect its origin, but an essential ingredient of any potential charge would be to find it in someone's actual possession or by an unequivocal admission by the prisoner. No chance – they would simply throw it out at the first sign of staff approaching and deny ownership.

Some drivers delivering supplies to the prison were very vulnerable and either through a misplaced sense of sympathy, greed to make money or as a result of even threats of violence made against themselves or their families, would fall victim.

Methods we have discovered have been wide and varied, amongst these are some described below.

Felt tip pens sent in for a prisoner's use with the ink rods shortened to insert drugs, pencils had leads shortened. One discovery was made of drugs hidden under a denture plate. Also, a prisoner with a glass eye had some secreted in the socket. Both extremely uncomfortable hiding place,s but some would go to any lengths to achieve their aims.

Hobbies being popular were used: for example, strips of foam rubber used for filling toys were slit open and the drug placed in and the foam resealed. Boxes with purpose built false bottoms. Under postage stamps or envelope seals. Sheets of perforated paper could hide doses of LSD, one dose per square, the methods were endless and success represented big money in prison. The most regularly used routes were via the various visits, incoming mail and property and of course by persons trafficking. The latter being the most used one. Constant vigilance was required along with the necessary pressure to create the desired deterrents.

The very well behaved, compliant and most polite prisoners were often the ones to be watched, because your mister nice guy could be the biggest dealer you had despite the fact that he was a model prisoner.

Even searching had its own headaches. If anyone is under an illusion that all prisoners are completely co-operative – forget it! Especially in top security establishments. Comments such as "Come on Guv, my tea's getting cold," referring to their evening meal, or "Don't you touch me down there, or I'll see my brief," were amongst the threats used to a keen young officer and designed to put them off a thorough search by threats of formal complaints.

Correct searching is vitally important and any distraction can result in a moments lack of concentration, during which time the concealed package could quickly be passed on to someone who had already been searched. This is simple to do because when I was tutoring new staff at the training school we used to pose as prisoners and as amateur as we were, we were able to pass items over to others without anyone having the slightest suspicion.

The more staff present during a search the better, but unfortunately;y manning levels did not always allow this.

Recently many debates have taken place relating to the uses of cannabis and its being legalised. If what they are talking about is making a sick persons quality of life better or even bearable, then I have no argument about this at all. I do however, object to any drug, especially class A, being legalised in a prison environment, because not only would this lead to separate class divisions because of money, or lack of it to buy.

it would also provide an in-road for excess profit-making and the potential for violence to erupt from the dealers and for more pressures to be put on by the dealers henchmen, not only towards people in custody, but also to family or friends of the person being pressurised.

I feel that drugs created an unsettling effect upon prisoners, because a shortage to a regular could mean danger to staff or other inmates. Take smoking for example, especially if someone is trying to give the habit up. The comments by the long suffering spouse is pleading with them to start again, because it's unbearable, so just imagine the havoc created by someone with a much more serious addiction.

Use of alcohol was a very different matter, because if a prisoner was drinking it, the tell-tale signs were much more obvious, they couldn't hide the smell on their breath, it was likely because of not using it regularly that they would be unsteady and speech could be slurred. Their actions ranged from stupidity to extreme violence.

Quite often those who had been on home leave would have had a few, but provided they were reasonable in their behaviour we would let them sleep it off.

A Nasty Experience

It all started with a telephone call. It was a Sunday and I was in charge. The caller from the Prison Department explained that the press was doing an article on open prisons which would appear in Monday's editions, but it was not specific to one prison, but just a generalisation. It's nothing to worry about the informant continued. Not so! As I was to discover when I called at the newsagent the following day: 'SEX, DRINK, DRUGS IN OPEN PRISON' so the headlines read, not only did it name our prison, but also it named staff and published photographs, taking up a full double centre page spread for three days. The nightmare didn't go away for us in three days, but lasted a full six months. So much for generalisations.

A team of police arrived, headed by a Chief Superintendent to carry out what turned out to be a lengthy enquiry. Staff homes were searched and the atmosphere was bad. The outcome was that despite the allegations – which incidentally came from a prisoner – no one was charged with any offence.

The investigation, serious as it was did have its lighter moments. One officer who had recently moved to a new home was alleged to have taken a large amount of draught excluder from a workshop in the prison. He said he had a large amount of this to the officer questioning him, this was followed by a team arriving to search his home. True, he had a large amount of draught excluder, but totally legitimately, also he was able to produce receipts to this effect, because he had acquired it from the builders as part of a package deal. At this stage the police wished to depart rather rapidly, but the officer seeing it as a huge joke offered them spades, saying that there may be something hidden in the garden. They had by now lost interest and beat a rather rapid retreat.

This period caused much tension amongst staff and was one best forgotten as a bad dream.

I found that when we needed support badly, some management didn't give it. I vowed that if ever I were faced with such a situation, I would be there to support them until anything to the contrary was proved. A lot of respect was lost during this period when all that was called for was a little feeling.

Whilst at Sudbury, I experienced a variety of people serving sentences including police, clergy, legal, doctors and many businessmen. At one stage we accommodated virtually the full rank structure of the police, not from the same force, but a chief superintendent, two inspectors, a sergeant and a constable. One of which was serving life and one who was sentenced just for a minor theft, just as he was coming up for retirement. All it was for was a couple of cans of lager, probably lost his pension and gratuity for what? Absolutely nothing!

My own personal feeling is that this is very sad when a person has given a whole lifetime to serving society, falls and loses everything because of petty crime.

I used to make a point of seeing any ex-police or prison staff. Particularly police and explaining that I had also been a policeman and appreciated how they must feel and if there was anything I could do to help them settle in, then I would, but they had been convicted in law and would receive no preferential treatment.This usually worked and they applied themselves to the system and survived through to discharge. Other prisoners knew when a policeman or prison officer had been sent down, 'bush telegraph', travels fast. The majority were accepted and apart from the odd jibe there was little trouble, only those who tried to throw their weight around came unstuck.

On several occasions we had our suspicions about a prisoner on the prison works department. He was the driver of a dumper giving him a fair share of freedom within the grounds. He was suspected of using the dumper to go and hide out, so we kept observations.

Following the afternoon work parade, true to form he collected his dumper and as it passed us we could see he had a mattress on board which confirmed our suspicions. We watched as he headed for the deer-keep, now disused and overgrown.

My colleague and I took a steady stroll down to the deer-keep where we found the dumper hidden away and tucked into the corner was this figure face down on the mattress, a tin of tobacco at one side and a radio blaring away on the other. I turned the radio down and said, "Good afternoon, I hope you are comfortable." His response of, "Oh Shit," was less complementary.

As we returned him to more secure surroundings we noticed that drawn on the mattress was a full-sized female figure, so he also had company!

On adjudications the following day he was ordered to be returned to closed prison where staff could keep a closer eye upon him and he would be less able to wander – we hope.

The Farm

Each weekday we sent a work party to the prison farm at Frankley under the supervision of two officers.

The farm was managed by full time staff comprising, farm manager, foreman, pig man, woodman and general farm hands. All employed by the Prison Department.

A massive area and twenty inmates despatched for miles into the fields made it somewhat of a nightmare for just two officers. Easy access to and from the farm made it easy to drop off parcels, or for a female to make herself available to her partner or indeed other partners, at a price of course. Plenty of woods and hundreds of hiding places, full time supervision was virtually impossible. It would be extremely lucky to catch anyone in the act. I am really talking of the minority, most of the party were pretty well behaved.

If an act of indiscipline occurred then the area was so isolated that it could become very threatening for staff.

I recall one such incident. I was orderly officer one lunch time when I received a rather desperate call from the officer with the farm party, he said that two men had been fighting with machetes, he had managed to separate them, but tempers were still frayed and he feared the consequence should they meet again.

I quickly arranged an escort of three and myself to attend and collect them. After arriving, the officer outlined the situation and I saw the two men, warned them that as they would be travelling back in the same van that they had better behave. They were each handcuffed to an officer and the two of us who were not cuffed sat between them.

I have never been so frightened in my life, and over the years I have covered many top security escorts and felt much more at ease. You would naturally think that the prisoners caused this fear, but they behaved perfectly. The whole return journey, some forty-five miles became an absolute nightmare. The responsible person was our driver, a dear man, but that trip I will never forget. He joined a motorway and virtually shook hands with a Buxted Chicken juggernaut, missed a halt sign and went straight over a roundabout. I am certain that the prisoners breathed a sigh of relief when we arrived at our destination. I know we definitely did.

Despite this I was privileged to have known him, and when he became terminally ill, I visited him at his request. He wanted some advice as to how to put his house in order and I felt very honoured to be asked t do this for him.

A Good Turn Out

During my tour of Sudbury I became responsible for taking charge of guards of honour at staff funerals, covering unfortunately too many in my time. All of these were as would be expected, very sombre affairs, with immaculate turnouts by staff.

There are some that leave a clear imprint, because of something out of the ordinary happening and strangely enough often amusing.

The first related to the van driver who took us out to collect the machete fighters.

Following the service, the guard of honour formed and the coffin was led to the hearse, the driver started the vehicle, so I gave a salute as the vehicle moved forward, or so I thought! It just stopped and the priest got out, he whispered, "I won't be a sec,' disappearing into his church. I remained in the saluting position. The second he said he was going to be was the longest one I have ever known. I'm sure he could have conducted another service, because my arm was slowly stiffening. My friend, I am sure if he was watching from above was certainly having the last laugh at my expense.

The second funeral took place in a small church in the suburbs of Derby. We arrived early for me to form the staff up on the path leading to the church doors. I had just briefed them and sited myself next to the church door, when to my horror I saw strolling up towards me a group of leather coated gentlemen, carrying musical instruments. They were a jazz band! I pleaded with their leader not to start up until I had given my words of command. Fortunately, he obliged, but only just, because no sooner had I called the staff up to attention, than a blasting rendition of, 'When the Saints', started up. I certainly do not recommend trying to give words of command with a jazz band sounding off. This was bad enough, but worse was to come. After the service the vicar thoughtfully played classical piped music and the jazz band played another tune and as for me I didn't march leading the coffin, I floated. Still, again I'm sure that our departed colleague enjoyed every moment, because he was a keen jazzman. These tales are just a few, there are many more.

Finally, no matter what grade staff are a unique feature of our job was that apart from work we often spent our break times together.

This particular day was no different, we had breakfast together, after which we used to play pool. This young man was a good player normally, but this particular day he excelled.

At lunchtime he went off duty to take over the duties of Night Orderly Officer that night, but by teatime he was dead. Killed in a road accident – only a young man with a very young family.

The farewell took place at a local crematorium and the staff parade was something he would have been proud of as an ex-soldier himself. Many times facing danger in active service and to die in this totally needless way. The following Sunday was Armistice Day and his wife, a cub mistress, bravely led her pack on parade, despite the traumatic experience she was about to face. It took great courage for her to do this.

Getting to Know You

During those days many staff tended to reside in quarters and social life revolved around the Officers Social Club. Regular entertainment was organised throughout the year and some really good events took place. However, the only problem was that despite the closeknit communities the conversation revolved around shop.

Everyone needs a break and it was a very welcome decision when staff were permitted to buy their own properties. Originally, the quarters were very close to the prisons, so should anything erupt within the prison – say a riot or a demonstration – then staff could be called and be on duty very quickly.

By purchasing further away, staff could still be called by phone and most have cars, so they could still get to the prison nearly as quickly.

The added bonus was that staff were able to integrate more with the mixed communities which, not only allowed officers to get to know the people, but it gave the community the chance to see that staff were not the two-headed monsters some though they were.

Generally officers took a part in the social life becoming involved in politics, religion, education and sport, and became an asset rather than a liability.

There are some very intelligent people in the service, and the days of the so-called 'Thick Warder' have long since passed, if indeed it ever existed at all.

Modern selection and training take care of this with particular emphasis being placed on teaching inter-personal skills.

Strange People

Many characters from all walks of life come into prison. I have met millionaires, tramps, lawyers and doctors. Whilst talking of one doctor, who was convicted of giving a lady member of his staff an aphrodisiac type drug to gain sexual favours.

for some reason, obviously best known to himself, he decided to lose his professional identity and carry out all the mannerisms of a con, ie: he wore the hat, smoked wafer thin roll ups and associated with the heavies. No trouble whatsoever, but strange to have disassociated himself from the life which he was normally used to.

Another who used to perform all manner of idiotic acts for smokes, who before going off the rails was well respected and a chief Draftsman until losing his wife. I used to say, "Why Roland, whatever would your poor wife think of you?" He would shrug his shoulders and say, "Well, she's not here is she." I thought a good job in some respects.

The silly tricks he would get up to would be letting other prisoners draw on his head, jumping into the goldfish pond or ridiculing staff.

Others would be so extroverted. One a very strong outgoing character displayed these traits from the time he entered my office. I asked him if he had any immediate problems, "Well yes, I have two. One I am worried about my jet airliner in France and the other about my castle in Portugal." I was about to explode and say, "I suppose you are missing a dinner date with royalty," and then laid into him for taking the mickey. However, I didn't, which is a good thing because all he was saying was true. He was a self-styled millionaire, making his fortune by introducing the garden gnome in a big way in this country.

After release he used to send me a Christmas card with a poem relating to Christmas and prison. One unique feature was that he could rapidly sign his signature which would be the exact replica of gnomes' head.

Musical talent was also present. We had one man who could go into the church and despite the fact that he did not read music, could perform the most haunting rendition of Beethoven's Moonlight Sonata on the organ which would echo through the open doors across the prison.

Another organist who this time could read music, in fact, it was his profession, displayed his skills in the village church. He was a Dutchman and played in Cathedrals over the world.

Finally, yet another organist, a funeral director, who was convicted of mis-managing funeral fees, by so many to his firm and then one to himself until he was found out.

All the above were in the main, nice people, who for reasons known to themselves had strayed.

Some, the most well behaved people I have ever dealt with, were the Derbyshire Miners during their strike. The majority were allocated to maintaining the prisons gardens and once they organised themselves the gardens were kept immaculately. In bloom they matched any display open to the public. They have won many awards for best kept gardens and have also made up the hanging basket displays for nearby towns.

Conversely, some of the worst behaved were from the younger section of the population. These had made the transition from young prisoner to that of adult status, sometimes happening overnight, and as such were unable to adapt to the sudden change, still full of life and mischief.

Quite often we didn't need to intervene, because they were controlled by the older element, who didn't want the aggravations. If we did have to step in, then more often than not we would have to resort to what was known in prison circles as the Ghost Train. This is usually carried out as an undercover move and takes place very rapidly. The idea is the prisoner being moved out is unaware until the very last minute, when he or she is quietly spirited away to pastures new.

The reality of the situation is that quite often they are aware of it via various sources. It could be that the tea boy is conveniently around when the persons cash and valuables are being collected and hears a name, or he is passing an office when the transfer is being arranged, or the reception orderly is aware that a certain prisoner's property and clothing is being packed and it doesn't take a few minutes to nip out on a fictional errand and pass the information on to the person being moved or someone who knows him and passes it on.

Often it would be welcomed by the one being moved out, the usual excuse would be that open prison was seen by them as a 'Soft touch', as I saw it however, was that they were unable to cope with self discipline and preferred someone to think for them.

In open conditions if someone is on hunger strike, it would be very difficult for us to be aware, but usually one of the other occupants would spot this and tell us. We would check this out and take action as appropriate. Usually, it was for a purpose, could be medical or mental or following a domestic dispute or as a protest. Often they would be admitted to a ward in the hospital where supervision could be maintained.

Oh! Him

Occasionally, we would have well known people serving a sentence from either the world of sport or entertainment and obviously the time would eventually arrive for their release. On the actual day press and TV crews would arrive at the gate lodge and wait for photos and interviews with them.

This is when we would put an alterative plan into operation by releasing the person either by taxi or private car out of another gate.

After this we would go to breakfast, as we passed the newshounds we would tell them that the person they were waiting for went out ages ago.

Their reactions and facial expressions were a sight to behold, when they realised they had been hoodwinked.

Sometimes a prisoner being released would face re-arrest on another charge, but effectively could not be re-arrested until they had left the prison gates, because until that time they were technically still serving the current sentence.

A prisoner did not have to be released first thing in the morning; they just had to go in time to reach their destination by nightfall.

I have actually seen a prisoner about turned and locked up for abusing the officer taking him to the gate and remained so until mid afternoon, when he made a full apology to the officer. He realised he was on thin ice, because all the Governor needed to do was to take some remission from him and he would not have gone out at all, and bang would have gone his reunion and his first pint.

On the gate arrest a prisoner must be given at least twenty-four hours notice and the opportunity to contact his legal advisor. We would judge the persons reaction and based on this would decide whether perhaps it would be better to move him to more secure accommodation, from where he would be less likely to abscond. Imagine the dance he could lead police officers from an open prison.

Discharge

The discharge routine would normally be carried out by a PO who was responsible for ensuring that the right person was the one being released, and that they were being released on the correct day with two exceptions. A person paying off a fine to secure early release or a person being ordered to be released following their appeal being upheld.

Also, you had to ensure that the person was in possession of all their property, including valuables and cash.

The prisoner was usually identified by his photograph and a few details of a confidential nature known probably only to him. This usually worked, but there are some exceptions, for example, identical twins. This actually happened and as with most twins, both knew the answers to most of the confidential questions. This left something of a dilemma – one brother unlawfully at large and one in custody unlawfully who must be released. Fortunately the one unlawfully at large was re-arrested fairly quickly and the other sent on his way.

The firearms act also applied to discharged prisoners who were banned from holding, acquiring or possessing any firearm for periods up to life depending on the length of their sentence.

Often the police would call us to give evidence if someone breached this rule.

Rules made are continually being broken and each prisoner who was released on any type of licence had to sign to say that they understood all the conditions, because for a breach of the rules they could be rapidly returned to prison.

Finally we had to ensure that the prisoner had no complaints. Some would try it on, but my answer was to tell them to return to the waiting room and I would investigate the matter. This worked miracles, because they didn't wish to be held up, they would say, "Forget it Guv, I'll write in." Which more often than not they didn't. If of course the complaint was genuine, it would be properly looked into, but eight out of ten were not. They were 'try ons'. This was a very important job and much attention had to be paid to it.

The Wanderer Returns

Not always voluntarily, for example, one evening I received a call to go to the gate, where an absconder had surrendered. Yes, he had surrendered, but not of his own free will. When I arrived his mother had him firmly by his ear lobe and had used her powers of gentle persuasion.

Another, who was out of time, as shown on his licence, he had been released to get married and was returned by his new wife – not only had he overstayed his licence, but he also apparently overstayed his welcome. She was starting married life the way she intended to continue. I thought, "Good luck to him".

Industrial Action

It's strange, because I have always supported the union, however, sometime you inadvertently become the proverbial 'Scapegoate'.

I refer to industrial action and the ensuing instructions I received which were that, as Orderly officer, I was supposed to order work parties from parade to work. I was to refuse to do this, it was added that I would probably face suspension, but not to worry, because we had good legal representation. My second in command was to do the same and the same fate was likely to befall him.

Over breakfast break we discussed this and decided that no way were we prepared to put our jobs on the line.

Returning, feeling somewhat down hearted we were stopped by the duty governor, who said he had heard what was planned and rather than us be placed in such a position, he was cancelling the work parade. I can assure you that we breathed a sign of relief.

Conditioning

The saying familiarity breeds contempt is a very true one especially in relation to this particular incident.

The scene was a top security wing in a small but extremely busy local prison.

Everything was self-contained, including the exercise yard. When they went onto the yard they were carefully monitored and the officer in command carefully reported his numbers to the control room, and the electronic locking system was released. All were high-risk prisoners.

Apart from exercise they would play sport and some would chat to staff.

During the course of the conversation, one prisoner asked if he could play a trick on the yards redband. The trick he explained was with a roll up (cigarette), tied to a piece of black thread. The idea was to throw this over the pathway and as the redband bent to pick it up this would be snatched away and no harm done. Just a bit of fun.

This prisoner selected a day when the Control Room was manned by a person he had began speaking to.

The redband – who incidentally is a prisoner trusted to work alone – walked past, saw the cigarette, bent to pick it up and, whoosh! It vanished, everyone burst into laughter. He shook his fist and wandered off.

What wasn't realised was that the string was not a joke but to register the distance between the security fence and the outer wall in readiness for a forthcoming escape attempt.

I say attempt, because it failed, the vaulting horse which they had intended to use as a ladder was not quite the height to reach the top.

The idea was there, people had been conditioned, it was just fortunate that the distance and height had been misjudged, that is fortunate for us.

The old saying, 'question the obvious', certainly applied here, because however innocent a practical joke appeared, there is often an ulterior motive lurking behind the scenes.

Manipulation be it in a big or small way is always part of a prisoners daily vocabulary.

full nude figures were not allowed on display in the dormitories, so on the inspections on Wednesdays and Sundays, cleverly made paper undies would mysteriously appear to cover the vital parts and after the inspection all would be revealed once again.

Inspections do not hold the same value today. No one in my time fooled around. The whole ritual took around ten minutes and if they chose to misbehave then we would simply return and carry out another in their time. They soon got the message.

With the arrival of lifers it had a tendency to stabilise the sillier element, because lifers had so much to lose.

Prisoners on the eve before reaching their release date were subjected to certain rituals. Some of which we didn't even know about, but one in particular we did. Despite numerous efforts to stop it, was still carried out regardless, this entailed throwing fellow inmates into the pond. The majority of times it happened was under the shadow of darkness, often when staffing levels were down to their lowest. Usually these rituals were not in good humour, but carried out by bullies wishing to flex their muscles. When the prison was handed over to the night staff there were only a limited number of patrols who could not be everywhere at any one time. What went on at night was anybody's guess. Kangaroo courts run by bullies, sitting in judgement on people who were probably weak-minded and certainly no worse than themselves. I found it despicable for them to issue out their own form of punishment. If they were caught they were dealt with severely, but catching them was the biggest problem. Once we received a plea to intervene in a nightly activity that was causing a great deal of concern. This involved the use of a 'Ouija Board', and visits from the spirit world. I think that the use of this type of object is frightening enough in the outside community let alone in a place that you are captive and cannot move.

Inter-dormitory night raids took place, usually using buckets of water, they would creep up to another dormitory in the small hours, saturating the area in water, light bulbs would be blacked out and trip threads placed at strategic intervals, mostly stretched across doorways. All designed to make creeping up and catching them in the act very difficult. To make it awkward for them we used to carry out extra inspections and property checks, in their free time, which had a deterrent effect because it probably took place in the middle of one of their favourite films or TV programmes.

Dormitories would change according to the type of occupants, one could be first class for a long time, then one or two disruptive characters are moved in and it becomes utter chaos. Often a timely word from their own colleagues would do the trick. On rare occasions staff would give up their free time to enable the inmates to see the end of a football match. The proviso that as soon as the game was over they would return to their dormitories to enable staff to go off duty because many had been on twelve hour shifts.

This went fine until some decided to kick the system and make sure that staff were delayed in getting off duty. Never again, was the comment and quite right this was.

The next time an application was made I made sure that they knew the reason why. It is not just prisons where this happens when a very small minority spoils everything for the majority.

Nowadays TV sets are installed in all dorms and there is far less hassle. A TV is said to take the place of an officer and I find this to be true.

Should a film bore them then the opposite applies, an example of this took place at Birmingham Prison when the film, 'The Music Man' was shown, not in retrospect the ideal film for this type of audience. This quickly became evident when Robert Preston started singing the song, '76 Trombones', chairs began flying around the darkened chapel. Luckily no one was injured and the alarm had been raised, we found the light switch and restored order. The inmates were given the choice to either behave or get out. A great many opted to leave which quietened the situation down considerably.

Trouble could quickly erupt when a large group was together, especially in a darkened area. One such event took place, again in the chapel, on this occasion a prisoner was badly slashed. His injuries were life threatening but fortunately for him a rapid medical response saved him.

Retaliation began when a prisoner thought to be the attacker received a nasty puncture to his eye. The big attack took place after both parties were discharged from prison, when a family feud erupted resulting in G.B.H. charges and members of both families being sentenced to fresh terms of imprisonment and the conflict continued.

It was an extremely dangerous world and as with most threatening situations required staff with three qualities to handle it; understanding, tact and above all experience. Prisoners are extremely good psychologists and can quickly recognise inexperience and will quickly exploit a situation if the opportunity arises.

Most of the latter being gained by service at a prison which dealt with every class of prisoner, both convicted and non-convicted, also every routine function in the day to day operations of the prison system. This is only found at one of the big local prisons. I am a firm believer that all new staff should be posted to a local prison before moving onto more specialised establishments. Such as those dealing with young offenders or with prisoners at other training establishments.

Telephones

In an attempt to allow prisoners to maintain domestic contacts it was decided to introduce the facility to use telephones, but with access restricted to making calls only. Being as we are suspicious by nature, there was a host of problem that we could foresee, such as what other devious uses would the phone be put to, planning an escape perhaps, further crime or arranging for parcels to be smuggled in or for placing bets. All of which were totally illegal.

The other problem we foresaw was of the stronger element manipulating the weaker and taking up most of the time allocated. The system was to be operated by an inmate orderly whose responsibility would be to allocate blocks of time to users and ensure they were strictly adhered too. Phone cards could be purchased via the prison shop or brought in by prisoners' visitors. The intention was to take an already heavy workload away from the probation and after care services, by making the prisoner responsible for much of his home contacts and sorting out his own problems up to certain limits of course.

If the problem was big, say a serious illness or big money problem, then of course the service would afford all the help possible. But if it was to see if his wife had returned home safely or something about a forthcoming visit, then these problems could be sorted out by the prisoner.

The only way the system was manipulated slightly, was for the benefit of prisoners working early mornings or late evenings – the kitchen staff or out-workers. The expected misuse of the phone did not take place very much and the facility saved any amount of problems, rather than unnecessarily worrying and festering inside which in turn could lead to aggression against staff or other inmates. If they could speak to their families they would probably clear the matter worrying them on the spot. This facility has now been extended to the majority of prisons and has been welcomed by most.

Like everything good, someone will try to take advantage by exploiting it, but the majority are grateful for being given the chance to speak with their families and friends.

A Fresh Start

At one stage staff in the service depended largely upon overtime to supplement their wages, consequently the budget hours rose enormously at tremendous expense to the Treasury. In the larger prisons some staff were actually doubling the salaries, but hours worked were taking their toll. So what happened was, that they were tired and despite dedication were lacking in efficiency and energy, consequently sickness increased.

Family life was suffering, children forgot what dad looked like and poor old mum shouldered most of the domestic responsibilities because husbands were too busy working overtime. The situation was becoming fairly desperate and the powers that be realised that they had to act quickly. A working party was set up and a new system known as 'Fresh Start' was introduced.

This system identified a great many problems, including staff grading, promotion structures and excessive overtime. It recognised the need for staff to spend more time at home and towards this end it introduced reasonable basic annual salaries. No longer would staff have to rely upon overtime to supplement their earnings, or should I say this was their hope.

If extra hours were accrued staff would have to take the time off in lieu. TOIL as it became know. Many staff didn't like this at all at the start, but as they looked more deeply realised its advantages. They could plan a fishing trip or a game of golf in advance or that holiday when the kids were off from school.

They could bargain with their group manager and strike a deal, perhaps someone who had gone off sick needed to be covered for urgently and the officer covering would probably offer to work the shift, provided he could take the time owed to coincide with his plans. Thus an amicable agreement was reached.

I would not wish you to think that each time the need arose the situation could be resolved as easily as that, but it created the platform upon which two people could work from and by skilful negotiations on both sides most situations could be resolved.

It abolished the Principal Officer and introduced Line Managers, such as Residential Group and personnel. The original Chief Officer grade was abandoned and the old Chiefs were offered a package deal to take early retirement or to join the Junior governor grades. Many of them took the money and ran.

I can't say I blamed them, because every uniformed service needs a figurehead and that's just what the Chief Officer was. I was given the job of Personnel Training Manager. A job that I viewed with some scepticism at first, for two reasons: I was to enter a field in which I had no previous knowledge and my new boss was a non-uniformed civil servant. So after twenty plus years of working with a uniformed Chief I was going to have to start all over again. As it happened he was great and taught me much about personnel management. I had two girls working with me and they not only guided me but got me out of several nasty situations. I found it was a whole different thinking process to what I had been used too. I also found that my in tray would n ever be empty, however much I tried.

Staff training presented no problem, I was always happy teaching. I was responsible to the Governor for ensuring that all was prepared for him to hear adjudications. That all charges were presented correctly and that staff and inmates were ready to give evidence. Excuses to delay hearings were not accepted, Governors were busy people with limited time to spare. I had a good understanding with my Governor, he said and I did.

Some Governors were cynical and comical with their comments. One prisoner when charged with being unshaven complained that the water was cold. The Govenor put his pen down, gave a chiselled stroke to his jaw, smiled and said, "Do you think that I have always had the luxury of hot water? I have shaved with ice water from a biscuit tin." He had been a pilot in wartime, winning the D.F.C. He winked at me, "Ensure he reports to you in ten minutes." the prisoner scooted off grateful that he hadn't lost remission. He did report back to me, a few scratches, but nevertheless, clean shaven.

When dealing with a more aggressive character who, in answer to the Governors question, replied "Bollocks", the Governor without even looking up asked, "Is that with one 'L' or two?" The secret was to refrain from grinning, although I must admit it was very hard at times.

On Stage

Each year prisoners would produce their own pantomime, usually under the direction of the Education Department and assistance from some willing helpers from local villagers.

Rehearsals began months before and having suspicious minds we wondered exactly what occurred behind the scenes during some of the time. The productions were of a high quality and usually coverage by the press attracted very favourable reports. The actors, getting their temporary rise to fame and the elderly and children loving it.

Some of the jokes and quips related to other inmates and staff, myself included. One particular sketch concerned a fairly well known heavy, who was playing the part of a beast in the jungle who was caged. When the leading man asked him how long he had been caged up for, he replied, "Seventeen years." I am sure that to this day he didn't realise that this quip was directed at the exact time he had served on this sentence, because I feel that had he have, he would have broken out of his cage and eaten him.

Prison has produced some excellent actors, several I know have gone on to start in various well known soaps and one on the classical circuit.

Besides actors, there have been some very good artists and writers. Each year a competition takes place nationwide to find the best artists and model makers for which prizes are awarded. To win an award in this competition was coveted by the entrants. One of the best I have seen was of a scale, working steam traction engine, one of the worst was supposed to be of Wolverhampton Town Hall. It actually looked more like the leaning tower of Pisa, before it eventually collapsed.

Model making was popular and we had to be very watchful, because Kings, Queens and Bishops tended to vanish from the communal chess sets and ended up gracing galleons and other models as figureheads.

Once, whilst I was taking daily applications, a prisoner serving a life sentence brought in a beautiful heart shaped musical box. I enquired who he wished to send it out to, but he informed me that it was for me, or at least for my young daughter. I accepted, but took it to the governor explaining the circumstances. His advice was to keep it, because it was very obvious that the man had gone through much time and trouble to produce it. We still have this on a dressing table at home.

It's strange sometimes, that people you wouldn't expect to show their feelings, actually do.

Going back to Onley, I recall that when my wife was taken into hospital prior to our daughter's birth. Not a single day passed when at least one boy didn't enquire how she was and on the day Ellen was born I was presented with a lovely hand made teddy for her. Uncle Bear, as he was named is still with us.

Some models had ulterior motives and the model makers had cleverly built in secret hiding places or sliding panels. Others had false bottom to conceal illegal items. If a prisoner handed out an item, it had to be carefully checked for hidden objects and even more so if the model was returned to the prisoner for repair. This probably would provide an avenue to smuggle contraband in under the guise that it required mending. They were up to every trick in the book, plus a few more I have no doubt.

Work

One of the jobs we used to provide labour for, especially during summer months, was maintenance at a number of Youth Hostels, that were set out amongst the beautiful Derbyshire Peaks. These were very popular jobs and much sought after by the inmates. We had to be very careful who we selected, apart from being trusted they had to be tradesmen, such as builders, carpenters or decorators.

They would be collected on each Monday and returned on Fridays. During this period they were unsupervised by prison staff and this is where I came in. As with all others, they were subject to Prison Rules.

My job was to ensure that they were complied with and that if they had any applications, to ensure they were heard and actioned, also to deal with outstanding problems.

Hostel staff were spoken to, ensuring they were satisfied with the prisoners behaviour and there was no cause for alarm with the community. I would be naïve, to say the least, if I believed that each night was spent in the hostels, because I am sure they joined in with the nearby villagers social lives, whatever that may be. I think this was accepted provided they didn't rock the boat.

I think that this was one of the most enjoyable duties I had in the service. There was nothing better on a nice summer's day, than setting out at your own pace and travelling around the Peak District visiting the hostels, all of which were set in renowned beauty spots in Derbyshire.

Attention Seekers

Of recent years much publicity has been given to suicides in prison, especially those committed by young people. The prison service has taken care in setting up a detailed monitoring system assessing those considered to be at risk, especially those with a previous history of making attempts on their own lives.

My experience is, that no matter what steps are taken, if a person intends to put an end to their life then eventually they will succeed.

An example of this was a very trusted orderly who, for no apparent reason, one lunchtime lunged at an officer with a pair of scissors. He was taken to a hospital room and anything with which he could cause harm to himself or others was removed. He was left dressed in pyjamas, the elasticated type and his toiletry articles. There was nothing else left in the room. His room was checked at very frequent intervals, however, he still managed to end his life. How? With his pyjamas, by forcing part of his pyjama trouser down his throat using the handle of his toothbrush to carry out the act.

How could anyone possibly have foreseen this happening – sheer determination. Such a waste of life, a budding author, who already had been published and had so much to live for.

On the other hand there were many attention seekers, people who slashed their wrists, but not making too much of a determined effort or cutting too deep. Others were firebugs, knowing that the staff would release them before any damage of a serious nature threatened them and those who would make a half-hearted effort to hang themselves. of course, the staff were not always available and by a quirk of fate things went too far by them paying the ultimate penalty.

These men, I fear, were making a cry for help and this was their only way of doing it, most of them had a sob story to tell and wanted someone to listen. Another type of nuisance, in trying to cause physical damage was the swallower. This character would swallow any available thing, from glass to metal. Many of these would aim to get taken to an outside hospital and possibly try to escape after treatment, or simply, just to get better food or extra visits. Things started to get serious when these individuals tried to swallow pieces of blades or needles.

I understood the medical staff to buffer the effect of the sharp points or edges used cotton wool. this was known as a 'Cotton Wool Sandwich'.

People tend to think that someone is mad to kill themselves, but I feel they are more desperate and very lonely than mad at the time.

Since I have retired I have taken to listening to Midlands late night radio and I am disturbed by the many people ringing in, who are openly stating that they wish to bring their lives to an end. The comperes of this programme make every effort to talk them round and get help for them. From what I can gather they are very successful, but compare this with a prison housing say, a thousand inmates. Just a voice in the wilderness with probably none of their peers listening, or even caring and staff so pressurised that they have no time for identifying this problem.

At least the radio provides the platform for people to air their problems and troubles to someone who can advise. There are people in the prisons willing to listen, but they are not able to mind read. The problem is not only restricted to prisoners, but also to prison officers. A spate of suicides occurred within the service one year and this in turn with illness, prompted the Home Office Prison Department to recognise that the problem of stress was becoming worrying, especially amongst the middle managers. These managers were able to recognise the problem in their staff, but not in themselves and when eventually identified, it was often too late.

Ischaemic heart disease was certainly amongst one of the chief offenders. I explained that at one stage I suffered a breakdown and it was for this very reason I volunteered to become a tutor on stress management. The courses I ran seemed well attended and people took the matter seriously when they realised that death could be the ultimate result. The type of work caused stress, staff were continually dealing with disgruntled customers who did not wish to be there in the first place in an artificial environment. People who if given the chance would cause havoc such as creating false alarms, fighting or constantly lodging complaints.

Lunchtime was the vital time, following a survey conducted at a top security establishment during which staff were fitted with electronic monitoring equipment. It was found that this was the period causing the most tension. Many pent up emotions were released by prisoners during this time, maybe, they had an altercation with authority, another inmate during the mornings work or were worried domestically or had received a 'Dear John', a letter from a loved one breaking off the relationship. Whatever the problem, the supervising officers were on the receiving end and inwardly expecting trouble.

A person would be foolish not to recognise signs and symptoms of stress and it was our job to try to help them identify these. The teaching certainly helped me enormously, during an emergency situation when an alarm bell was rung, all available staff would attend, not knowing what would confront them as they arrived. It could be someone in trouble, or just a false alarm as it so often was. The adrenalin starts to flow, true or false, and if this is repeated too many times the body's resistance breaks down, leading to sickness or worse.

All of us have different stress levels, some are able to absorb more than others. A sure path to disaster is to create too many stresses at once, for example, move home, change job and he wife being pregnant all at the same time. Not many can take this series of stresses at once.

Relaxing and enjoying what you are doing is the simple remedy. Listening to tapes or records, taking a bath or pursuing a hobby, gentle exercise. I found that reading helped my own problem. A book I recall just simply revolved around the humdrum activities of a village and of the day to day happenings within. Nothing startling, just simple everyday things that seemed to take me into their world.

Overcrowding

A major concern which constantly faces the Prison Department and one which can easily cripple the system is overcrowding. This creates a great many problems, for example, finding enough accommodation to house the extra inmates, having to utilise old army camps or disused buildings – see Morton Hall.

A few years ago the experts predicted a population explosion reaching 49,000, this has now increased dramatically and the fear is of 80,000 plus. Such a vast increase creates many problems. I feel an overcrowded prison is not a healthy or contented one – tension builds up – just imagine yourself attending an exhibition with just a few people in the centre. You're happy, having space to move around when all of a sudden, the visitors increase tenfold, you become irritable, not being able to move when and where you wish. Well, this is identical to the reaction of prisoners when others are crowded in. Staff are unable to devote as much time to the prisoners as before, pressure is on with more people to feed and clothe, more work is needed to occupy prisoners, visits may have to be shortened. Many more demands are made on the same number of staff and personal space becomes limited. There are still only the same number of hours to each day, although it makes you wonder with the increased workload.

Different non-custodial forms of punishments have been introduced with a view to alleviating the problem, but the majority have seemed to produce a knock on effect. Examples are suspended sentences, parole, probation and community service orders, but the end result is breaches of the order and ultimately many returns to custody.

This isn't new, because during the Second World War many prisoners were released to enlist, hence the population decreased dramatically until the mid forties, when once again up it went.

So is there an answer? I feel not. No matter what we try to do there will always remain a number of people who will return to prison. officers will never be out of a job, there will also be a group who must be held in custody – people who have committed serious crime like murder, rape, violence and those offending against the state.

Maybe we hold in custody a certain element who need not be detained – theft, non-payment of monies, shoplifters, etc., but the question is where do we draw the line.

Justice must be seen to be done, no one who offends in any way whatsoever, should ever be left thinking that they are getting away with it.

They must be made to pay, emphasis on the must. Enforcement orders must be carried out, even if it means taking money from earnings, savings or state pay-outs. So many times, people who are fined have no intention of paying, this is just not on, so I feel that a more severe method of enforcement must be employed.

Race Relations Liaison officers

To most of us the very mention of Race Relations is a subject which most try to avoid. This was my opinion as I entered the Governors office.

The service has to appoint Race Relations Liaison officers and you have been appointed. I wasn't asked, but told. I had to attend a course and take it from there, I was also instructed to give all staff some training in the subject, because all officers were expected to become involved. I was just the go between and trouble shooter between the system and the inmates.

I wasn't too happy, thinking, lumbered again, but reflecting upon it I found it to be a very interesting and absorbing subject. I learned much about all the customs, practices and diets of the various countries, their festivals and fasts and visited all the different places of worship, attending some of their feasts.

Training some of the staff was probably the most difficult issue to tackle. You had to make the course as interesting as possible, sometimes even light-hearten, but at the same time get over the message of equality between all races and the services policy relating to it.

It is proving its value over and over again in our ever-increasing, multi-cultural society, in our case, especially for people in prison.

In the course of our visits to the temples and mosques, we had to abide by their rules, part of which was to enter barefoot in the mosques during prayer. After prayers we asked the Iman why barefoot? His answer, whether true or not was, "when people walk along the street they tread in all sorts and I for one do not wish to touch my head in prayer onto the carpet, if someone had trodden into some dog or cats left-overs." Makes sense doesn't it. Neither would I, even if it wasn't strictly the true answer.

Another time, an Indian high Commissioner was relating an old Indian saying, "Never walk in front of a policeman or behind a donkey, both times you will get kicked!" this was very true also.

Part of our job was to submit an annual report, which broke down the various statistics relating to the general activities in the prison within the field of Race Relations. The subject I was reporting on was relating to work and education.

I wrote something like, "The daytime educational classes were well attended and included a large membership of the prisons West Indian population."

The report was returned to me and read, "the daytime education classes were well attended, especially by West Indians with large members." Maybe true, but not what I wished to convey to the Race Relations Board.

I found that the position was best not advertised too widely because if advertised too much, a certain nucleus of the population would certainly find something always to complain about, just for the sheer hell of it. The R.R.L.O. was on hand if problems arose and very quickly was sought out by either staff or inmates to rectify them. Many times the problem could be resolved quickly and efficiently by enlisting the co-operation of the parties involved. For example, during the feast of Ramadan, the participants ate two meals after sunset and before sunrise, so naturally had to leave the dormitory area during the small hours when other prisoners were sleeping. Thus disturbing them, making tempers rise, a compromise had to be quickly reached. So a calculation of the observers of this feast revealed that they could all be absorbed in a single dormitory, keeping all sides happy for the duration of the feast. Mostly the problems thankfully were minor, easily redeemable. It was the big things that could lead to riot or violent situations that we feared. Especially bearing in mind the ongoing race riots that at that stage were springing up all over the country.

Generally however, I found most inmates of whatever race, colour or creed were able to get along with each other reasonably well, which really was all we could expect.

Christmas

Christmas it is said is a time during which everyone should relax and enjoy themselves – or is it? Not exactly everyone, because in prison Christmas is a period which many prisoners – especially those serving long term sentences – choose to forget.

Deprivation of liberty means deprivation of the company of their loved ones and friends. They are given the option to hang decorations and display cards or they may just let it quietly slip by. Prison authorities try to make the period as tolerable as possible.

It begins with a multi-denominational carol service, to which all are welcome, including staff, their families, local inhabitants and of course the inmates after which the whole assembly have coffee and mince pies. The inmates are also given the chance to meet and talk with staff families.

Behaviour from the prisoners has always been impeccable, in fact, I have seen much worse in my own town church during midnight mass from the youth who couldn't hold their drink.

The only thing I used to dread was being asked to read a lesson. Teaching I found no problem with, but reading biblical script I found awesome, especially to the sea of faces, amongst which were probably a third of my charges, just waiting for the slightest slip which provided them with a talking point for the next few days. "Not bad Guv, but."

Sports and games were well organised and winners would be awarded prizes. The television provided much of the light entertainment and certainly did the work of another officer. Food was excellent, the chef providing traditional fayre and catering for the minority diets. Most people had more than their fair share of food. As the days wore on some became bored and quite regularly fights would break out, especially amongst the youngsters. This is where the P.E.I.'s would help considerably, by allowing them to channel their frustrations into physical pursuits. Discipline officers tend to joke about P.E.I.'s but in truth they were invaluable.

New Year's Eve would be monitored, especially for hooligans going too far. Senior staff tried to show a supportive presence during the change from the old to the New Year. Friendly rivalry was to some extent accepted, but we came down very hard on those who went over the top. You may say, why should they receive this sort of treatment? After all they are in prison! To this I agree, but most of them are family people and have feelings. Their families have done no wrong, especially children, so we tried to lighten the burden as much as possible.

Also, staff who are on duty have loved ones and children, so if the prisoners are kept content there is less likelihood of disruptions. Use of the telephone has helped this considerably.

During this period considerable vigilance is necessary and the incidents of absconds tends to rise. On impulse and hang the consequences, let's go home. The aftermath of course is loss of remission so most realise it just isn't worth it.

Espirit de Corps

On the many occasions when difficult situations arise it is remarkable how the staff who are going to deal with them unite together.

The emergency could arise for many reasons, both desperate and dangerous. No matter what it is, I have always found the officers and sometimes the administration staff enthusiastic at carrying out the job in hand and socially compatible.

The dangerous part would be guarding top security prisoners, who, if given the chance, would escape using whatever means they considered necessary, including violence. i refer to such people as the 'Train Robbers' or who are political or state enemies and of course rioters.

These were times when you needed a closely knit staff, who knew each others responsibilities and could act as a team in the event of an emergency. It could be, knowing how they would restrain a violent person, or how they would cover vulnerable areas in the event of an attempted escape, or just the sharing of intelligence information. Whatever it was, it was vital that they were able to work together. The disturbance directly need not come from the prisoners, it could come from relatives or even the public, especially if the offence had attracted much publicity.

I recall once, where we had to escort a prisoner into the court and having to walk down a fairly long path. This turned into, 'Running the Gauntlet' because, I think, the staff had as many umbrellas rained down upon them as the prisoner, who was a particularly nasty child murderer.

It was our job to protect such people. Another related to a man charged with the murder of a police officer. We took him to court and whilst awaiting his appearance, held him in the cells below. Whilst there three C.I.D. officers came and said they would take over whilst we had a cup of tea. Can you just imagine the possible result should we have accepted this offer? No thank you! I liked my job too much to have finished up queuing at the labour exchange.

As escorts we were issued with a document called a route form and with any special prisoners, special endorsements were written, on this particular one written in large red letters, 'On no account is this man to be let out of any officers sight.'

Riots usually result in many small incidents of disruption, happening in different parts of the prison and often call for small teams of officers to deal with them. Despite the fact that they are small, they can often be very violent and need handling with extreme caution.

riots are usually led by two or three so called ring leaders, and the remainder follow like sheep and really would prefer not to be involved.

Given the opportunity, these are the people to talk to, because without this support the ringleaders support is likely to breakdown.

The desperate point of my introduction of this subject refers to setting up a new prison as a temporary measure to help combat over-crowding as the chapter dealing with this will explain.

It would be wrong for me to say that I enjoyed such times, but probably, more appropriate to say that I appreciate the team spirit and the atmosphere that existed from those involved.

SIX DAYS TO DO IT

Morton Hall

Morton Hall is a stately building in the heart of the beautiful Lincolnshire countryside. It is steeped in history, but its main claim to fame is that during the Second World War, it became the base from which the RAF operations were planned. Military advisors used the building as an operational HQ.

The hall is situated in ninety acres of its own grounds. After the war it became a borstal training establishment. To commemorate its wartime connections, the two borstal houses were named after two RAF heroes, namely Sgt John Hannah, who was in fact the youngest recipient of the Victoria Cross and Guy Gibson, a legend in his own right.

Most recently the buildings were used for housing Vietnamese boat people and it is from here that I became involved.

I was called up by my own establishment and advised that, due to extreme overcrowding in the larger prisons, Morton Hall was to be reopened. This was to take some of the overspill, so I, along with other colleagues were to report there to assist in its preparation.

We arrived at the establishment where we were directed to the Chief Officers office. This was sited along with other offices covered by a glass-topped roof, giving it the appearance of a huge glass house.

Chiefs were a special breed by tradition, and always gave the impression of being completely unapproachable, until you were in trouble.

There is always an exception to every rule and this was one. He did not match the stereotype at all. Looking through his window I saw a man, not too tall with a goatee beard and rimless specs, looking more like an academic than a Chief. However, I was soon to find that he was through and through a Chief. He knew his job, was afraid of no one and backed his staff completely. I was proud to have worked with him.

The Chief introduced himself to us and then introduced us to the governor, equally a gentleman. Together they explained the project, which was ultimately to accommodate 150 category 'D' inmates, but the place was to be up and running within 6 days, t his was the deadline, impossible! Once again I was proved to be wrong.

My part in this was as the Unit Line Manager. To be responsible for ensuring that the prisons living area was fully furnished, including all the necessary stores from shoe polish to sheets. Ensure all stationery, printed forms etc., necessary to run a prison wing was at hand. That contingency plans were drawn up to cover everything from fire evacuation to absconds. Wing staff details prepared, plus of course, all the little niggles such as dripping taps, toilets not flushing, light bulbs not functioning etc., etc. I also needed to be available to listen if my staff had any problems and to act appropriately.

Initially an inspection of the living area was necessary, this revealed a total shambles, filthy to the extreme and should you be scared of creepy crawlies then forget this project, because they emerged from everywhere, who could blame them! They were entirely set-up from the time the building was left and objected to being disturbed. what had been left was indeed in need of replacing or renewing, nothing remained of any use.

Looks like we had a massive job on our hands – 6 days indeed, they must be joking.

Time to start in earnest, no chance of the luxury of an evening off. Straight down to work, deep cleaning. Ranks didn't enter into the equation. The usually smart black uniform disappeared to be replaced by boiler suits. First a check all around to see what we could discover which would help us to become – shall we say – the tidiest village. People certainly became experts at handling scrubbing brushes. whatever the task we were all striving to complete the operation in 6 days. Every member of staff worked their fingers literally to the bone.

Each night we all returned to our digs tired, but happy, and meeting the challenge slowly. Once again talking over the days happenings over a well-earned pint. Much of the equipment was either begged, borrowed or sometimes shamefacedly stolen. Night raids discovered all sorts of hidden treasures in places we didn't know existed.

Daily each department had their own problems, some more than others. Organising something like this is always going to be fraught with problems.

In prison it is said that there are three vital things that will keep a prisoner happy – 1) mail, 2) visits from family, and 3) food. A very prominent part of prison diet is home baked bread, eaten on the day it cannot be beaten, but kept any longer it tends to rapidly go stale. I'm no cook, much to my good lady's disappointment, but even I know that to bake bread, efficient ovens are needed and that was something else we didn't have. The cook tried, but unfortunately the result was catastrophic, the timely intervention of the local Fire Brigade saved us from further damage. Our ovens needed repairing or replacing, both of which take time, a commodity of which we did not have much of.

Progress was being made, all staff working as a team and maintaining a good all round sense of humour. At this stage I possessed the only internal telephone, as you can well imagine, this piece of equipment was used constantly and I saw many battles fought over the telephone. All the staff worked with a sense of purpose, determined to meet the goal.

Lunchtimes were spent by most of us in the local hostelry and over the period many decisions were made over a pie and a pint. People tended to be able to speak their minds without the formalities.

The buildings were already taking on a 'lived-in' look rather than the drab desolate appearance of when we first arrived. Supplies of food stuffs and other essentials were collected on a daily basis by the caterers who departed with an unladen three ton lorry, visiting the various prisons and returned loaded to the hilt. They had often managed to scounge other items which would be of use in the day to day running of a prison.

As you can imagine many humorous events occurred during their travels. One such incident happened when they were out purchasing bread in bulk in a nearby supermarket. Several people were being inquisitive; addressing remarks to each other to the effect that, why on earth were these men buying all that amount of bread. This conversation was loud enough for our boys to hear. So not to be outdone our group returned the conservation to each other, remarking that it was a good job that they heard about the bread strike. Suddenly bread became an extremely attractive commodity and the sales rose very rapidly. At least the supermarket manager was very grateful.

Back at the camp progress was being made, we were unearthing things from the numerous outbuildings which could be put to use such as old tables, chairs and even a washing machine. As you can imagine ninety acres held a whole wealth of hidden treasure.

The officer to be responsible for receiving the prisoners made good use of this, part of his responsibility was to ensure that prisoners own clothing was clean for their eventual release. He also made a good job of officers' shirts. Another great chap, he had a knack for achieving the seemingly impossible and we owed much to him.

To cover the grounds the Governor used a pedal cycle, and when the cats away the mice would play. So when he was off staff used his cycle, but there was always the danger he would pay an evening visit. This particular day someone used the cycle to patrol the grounds and returned with a punctured front wheel. With us being versatile we rapidly converted the office into a cycle repair shop and no one was any the wiser, luckily for the culprit, and my finger points no further than the reception officer.

One of the Governor's favourite habits was to ride around the living accommodation on his cycle fully cycling with a clear sign indicating that he was the 'Number One'.

You would have imagined this would raise a laugh. Not at all – prisoners would approach him with dead pan faces, as if he had just walked in on his morning rounds – one consolation was that he amused the staff.

The grounds, extensive as they were, over the years became overgrown with every imaginable weed merging into tangled masses and very untidy. However, as progress was being made many beautiful plants were discovered, including a delicate lacy pinky/white rhododendron. I carefully took a cutting of this, taking it and planting it at home. It flowers every year, in ten years it hasn't grown much, but it's very presence serves to remind me of the good times spent whilst setting up this new regime.

Some staff were keener than others and jobs being completed as quick as lightening, no sooner than you had turned your back something else happened. An example of this happened when someone paid a visit to the toilet, finding to his horror that whilst performing his call of nature, •someone had nailed up the door despite the protests being made by the

---

* See illustration eleven "Someone had nailed up the door despite the protests"

occupant. fortunately, the person inside had a two way radio and was released from his predicament fairly rapidly, however, such an incident wasn't quickly forgotten and the ditty about the two old ladies locked in a lavatory became suddenly popular, although I might add not to the unfortunate person who was so placed in this predicament.

Whilst there during one evening an elderly American gentleman arrived, asking to see the person in charge. He told me he was re-visiting the place, explaining that he was the flag officer during the period when the Dam Busters raid was being planned. He was fascinating and he explained in some detail the means employed, and the plotting involved in locating and keeping observations on the enemy and of its movements, especially tank movements.

As with all stately homes, ghost stories emerge in abundance, two of which spring immediately to mind, both have no connection with the halls previous occupants, but relate to wartime.

The first involved just sounds, which they say happen at night. It is supposed to start with car doors being slammed and an exchange of conversation, then the car moving off. Sounds straightforward doesn't it! The only problem is there is no car and no one around. Just sounds!

The second according to the villagers, involves a young man in the billets, who was awakened from his sleep by a man asking for an aspirin to ease his headache. The man in bed turned to his locker to get him one but when he turned back, no one was there!

The explanations given were, in the first incident, a young pilot and his girlfriend had been fatally injured after returning from a night out. the second, a young pilot had been killed whilst returning from an operation flight, and had previously lived in this billet.

These are only stories related to me by locals, how true I don't know, creepy through and I didn't intend to search for explanations.

We decided that people who lived within the area were entitled to know what to expect, and be re-assured that we weren't going to house violent or sexually motivated criminals. In the course of our tour we came across a cottage occupied by an old lady, we started explaining the nature of our visit to which she assured us that she was not concerned in the slightest about prisoners. She invited us in to show us why. As my colleague prepared to enter he quickly retraced his steps. The whole area was policed by geese. I then fully understood why she feared no one.

Another resident living nearby was the owner of a very large pig farm, the smell was enough. I don't think that any self-respecting prisoner would venture anywhere near the locality of this establishment. At times the wind conveyed this message very clearly, even to where we were based.

Many of the local inhabitants welcomed the re-opening of a prison. For some it meant trade. Whilst we were there the pub definitely did a roaring trade.

We would eventually need teachers, administration staff, night patrols and skilled tradesmen.

Also the chances were that the housing market would pick up, because of new staff being posted permanently to Morton Hall, who would want homes. So instead of having to turn their collars high they were made very welcome.

Despite the huge drive put in by all staff, the deadline was just around the corner and we were still beset by problems, one of the major ones probably was the absence of beds. No beds and the whole operation would fall flat on its face and all the staffs' enormous effort would have been in vain.

As I have told you I was still the main base for telephone communications and I was privileged to have witnessed some very high-powered negotiations and manipulations take place.

After numerous telephone calls the problem apparently was caused through some authorisation paper not being signed. It was pointed out that this was a necessity and very urgent. The person on the other end of the line apparently seemed so unconcerned until one of our most senior staff pointed out to him that this was an emergency measure introduced by the Government, and if they did not arrive on time the minister concerned would most definitely require an explanation, and we would have no option but to inform the minister as to who was responsible.

As if by magic the beds did arrive on time, but only just. They arrived on the evening before the first batch of prisoners were due. So again it was all hands on deck. Even the ladies from the offices helped, by the end of the day we all know how to use bed spanners. That night none of us went home early, but I'm sure the prison governor breathed a sign of relief because without everyone pulling together the operation would not have succeeded. He was so grateful that afterwards he supplied a crate of beer to down the dust. Yet another disaster avoided.

For posterity it was decided to have a group photo taken so we all dressed up in our Sunday best and posed before the camera, after which we were assured of a copy and a copy of the newspaper in which the photo along with a published article would appear. Alas, the gremlins struck once again. Not the ovens this time, but the camera which is supposed to have malfunctioned. If you ask for my opinion, I have a sneaking suspicion that it didn't have any film in!

The only thing I can rely on is my cutting of the rhododendron as a reminder of the challenging, but happy time spent setting up Morton Hall.

Personally, I felt this to be one of the most satisfying experiences of my whole career.

The big day dawned and we started looking around for any potential problems Is there sufficient toilet paper? Do we have the right books to take daily applications in? Are there spare light bulbs? Is the fire evacuation procedure clearly explained? Will they understand the daily routine? I could go on and on, but it appeared that my staff had taken care of every eventuality. I was still doubtful that we had missed something, but no, nothing appeared amiss. We had met the deadline with time to spare. The following day we began to fit into the prison routine, it was just as if we had been operating it for ages. Start with a check of the role – one down already – not a bad start out of twenty. A quick cup of tea and then hear the applications. There was a good proportion that needed advice or required some item or other. Although I managed the unit my powers were limited to issuing extra letters, allowing inmates to spend a set amount of their own personal cash, to change work (not applicable yet), and to change diet or to transfer. Other more important issues were for the Governor to deal with, such as being released to attend a funeral or visit a sick relative in hospital. To spend more cash than I was allowed to authorise, say over £100. To hear complaints relating to staff, something which I was not allowed to hear.

It was a mans right to go directly to the Governor without his even giving me an insight into the complaint. After all it might have been a complaint about me. Which it quite often was. Many of our guests did not like the word 'No', and some of the requests were preposterous, for example, prisoners were permitted to write some letters at public expense, these were called special letters. This particular man always wanted more. "Good morning sir, I would like twenty-two special letters." "Good morning, as I'm feeling generous you can have two," and I added, "you can purchase two extra from your private cash." "Two will be plenty," he replied. Quick change I thought, from twenty-two. They may ask for permission to have some creature comfort, they were not allowed to have such as chewing gum or a hot water bottle, late night TV after permitted hours. Usually if you were wise the answer would be 'No', because if you gave in you could create a precedent and they would take it as a right. All applications had to be handled with extreme care. To some it would be from genuine concern and others just a try on.

Also, on applications we would have those who were trying for the best jobs. Some for their own ends, others because they were genuinely keen. We preferred to select because quite often your hand picked orderlies turned out to be the best informants. They were an essential part of prison life because you could receive prior information relating to say, someone who was going to be beaten up or people who were extorting money from others under threat of running rackets. Much of my information relating to underground activities had been received via informants, in so called, 'perk' jobs, because it was normal for them to be in close contact with staff and none of the others took any notice when they were seen talking with officers, whereas other prisoners would immediately fall under suspicion if seen talking to officers and could fall into lots of trouble.

Every morning without fail there would always be a few regulars. I'm sure that as they woke up they would think, what can I see him for today? They were in the queue daily from Monday through to Friday, and if they didn't turn up you would get concerned, although on a bad morning you could happily strangle them.

All needed handling very carefully because more often than not this is where many of the explosive situations would erupt.

As time moved on, most settled but we still had the nucleus that were determined that they were not going to stay. When this happened we would arrange the prisoners return on a 'one to one' swap, with the sending prison, if they were set on not staying then this was in their interest and I might add ours as well. The only problems were that as you get rid of one troublemaker he was replaced by a worse one.

The aim was for us to take an intake weekly, until we reached capacity and with us nearly having completed our stay, the new staff would soon be arriving. Some of the auxiliary and night patrol staff was recruited locally, which gave us an additional task of interviewing applicants for the posts.

We advertised for night patrol officers and one of the applicants had retired from the prison service recently, he had the same rank as myself. A difficult interview took place, it was decided to appoint him to the job, not to my mind the most ideal, having held an in-charge position but democratically he was selected.

On his first night he tried to retain the authority he had previously held but quickly came unstuck, finding that he was just the same as the other night patrols and that his power was strictly limited to that of the others. The night orderly officer had the authority and quickly put the man right as tactfully as possible.

When I returned to my own prison the night patrols were working well as a team. Alas, he has since died.

Another task was to sit with others to allocate prisoners, to labour, we tried to put them where they would be most useful, but sometimes despite all our efforts, square pegs had to be wedged into round holes. Like outside some skilled or semi-skilled men were allocated to jobs that they were fitted to, however, others had to work at the less attractive jobs, credit to most of them, they knuckled under and worked extremely hard. Especially those working on the outside.

Most of us had a heavy heart because they had been good times and if you want to see comradeship in the service then the finest example is when an emergency situation arises. Secretly however, we were glad to be returning to our wives and families.

The lunchtime of the final day was spent as usual in the local; it was a light-hearted affair, a few speeches, plenty of chatter followed by two presentations.

The presentation was to the senior caterer and what better than a bright red toy fire engine to commemorate the episode of the ovens. The other presentation was to me and I would think you have guessed what I received. That's right, a bright red toy telephone complete with its own bell. It's certainly not going to have the same atmosphere at Sudbury.

I treasure my letters of thanks from both the Chief and the Governor, and feel their examples of leadership reflected upon us all.

Finally, I must not neglect my own staff; they were a tower of strength during what were extremely difficult times. I could always rely on them and of their uncanny knack of smelling out problems before they even arose. Whatever broke, there was always one of them able to fix it. Many of the things they did were far beyond their job descriptions.

So another sojourn comes to a close, another valuable lesson in organisation, something more to write about in my book. That is if I ever get round to writing one.

TEACHING TRICKS OF THE TRADE

A Chance I Had

The opportunity I had always wished for arrived very soon after taking up this new post.

Due to increased recruitment, the prison service was opening a temporary training school and I had been selected to take a part in the National Training Programme. The venue was Lancashire Police Headquarters Training School. We had been loaned a number of training rooms and a large office area.

My home during that period of time was to be a small hotel in Southport. I had taken part in local and regional training many times before but never at national level. Therefore, like others in the team I needed some guidance. We paired up and fortunately my colleague had more experience of training at national level.

In the initial stages most of the work involved hours of photocopying and organising timetables so that nothing clashed with other classes. The rooms had to be organised so that we didn't get any last minute hitches – which we did. One good thing, the Police Club was adjacent to our offices and quite often future plans were made over a pint.

There wasn't much time to spare and we were working fast and furious to meet the deadlines.

The courses were scheduled to last for nine weeks each and initially, at least for the first half we were to concentrate on inter-personal skills. This being a very important part of prison officer training it included showing recruits how to recognise tell tale signs such as, guilt, depression, hostility or fear by general body and eye movements ie. muscles twitching, especially neck muscles, over talkative, withdrawn and argumentative, all give out indicators to staff as to what might happen and to prepare them for it.

This was interspersed with physical education and control and restraint techniques.

The second half of the course dealt with much of the theory and practical side of a prison officer's duties also, first aid, radio procedures, race relations and AIDS lectures.

That being the 'nuts and bolts' of the course we prepared to receive the first intake of trainees and let battle commence.

Applicants for the prison service come from all walks of life but a large number are from the armed forces. Each team of class tutors was allocated between 20 and 30 students for whom they were entirely responsible throughout the entire nine weeks.

They became not only tutors but also father confessors and guardians. I have seen several grown men reduced to tears because of uncertainty or domestic situations. To a large extent we could empathise, because both trainers and trainee were being thrown together under artificially created conditions and away from their homes. However, this did not prevent us from giving a proverbial 'boot up the backside' should it be needed.

Sometimes students from other classes felt they could relate better to another tutor other than their own and visa-versa, we encouraged this.

The registration and induction day was very busy indeed, no chance to get to know anyone, it was like a continual conveyor belt. Interviews, allocation of rooms, kitting people out with uniform 'that's a perfect fit,' whether it was or not. Last minute phone calls, people opting out, break downs, forgotten to do something and domestic problems.

One lad I recall looked a bit like a 'dago,' neckerchief, earrings and a very casual approach. After interviewing him I gently hinted that as he was in a uniformed service he could perhaps moderate his style of dress down to a more sober tone. He assured me that I had no worries, I didn't. On his first day on the Parade Square he was immaculate from top to toe. Usually on the first day in uniform we allowed some leeway but he didn't need any, he must have been up all night preparing.

Following the parade we had what was known as a 'creeping death,' where everyone, including the instructors gave a brief introduction about themselves. This particular young man had just completed a lengthy period serving as a drill sergeant in a food guards regiment.

In later conversation I was to discover that his style of dress gave him an outlet from the ceremonial uniform he was generally used to. He was invaluable to me by giving up his spare time to take those who had no idea of marching and bring them up to standard. In addition to this he became a good student who in my opinion would make not only a good officer but also a potential leader.

Object lesson, 'never judge a book by its cover.' My first inter-personal skills lesson. Never stereotype.

Whilst at the training school, being a police headquarters you would think that all would be safe – not at all. For some reason best known to the person in question someone had an attraction for drinking mugs – especially unique ones, we lost a number of them. Many being mugs relating to favourite football teams. My first thought was that perhaps we should begin to collect helmets! Strange how some minds work.

The morning routine began with an inspection and a march off into the classrooms – one group starting the day in the gymnasium for physical education or control and restraint training, because this gave us good indicators as to students' determination, team spirit and courage.

Many practical exercises were created when the students least expected them, they were designed to test re-actions and reporting abilities.

We tended to set up situations between ourselves. For instance, on one occasion I was lecturing to a class when the door burst open and in walked a very irate tutor from another class. He grabbed hold of me saying "listen, you four eyed bastard, if you take another chair from my class I'll wrap it round your head." We would then start to fight. The act was so realistic that students would jump up to break up the fight. At this point we would stop and instruct the class to report on the incident, which they had just witnessed. For the first couple of times we would catch them unaware questioning our pedigree but afterwards they always remained alert and ready to report. This was of course the object of the exercise.

All of the practical exercises became extremely popular, however, no amount of simulated incidents could show them what it was like in reality, we could only prepare them.

Sometimes simulated incidents were overplayed. Attending another course were a group of high ranking police officers who were grouped around watching one of our exercises, mocking up a prisoner 'sit down' on a prison exercise yard. They were intrigued after seeing one of the course members with his left arm outstretched run two steps forward and one step back, zigzag, stop at the tree and start whistling. After a couple of minutes he carried out the same routine as before.

The police officers curiosity was aroused, they asked him what on earth he was supposed to be doing. His casual reply was, "I'm a dog handler and the dog wanted to pee." Shooting off, zigzagging on his way, leaving the group open-mouthed, probably thinking that all prison officers were mad.

One morning upon our arrival we were approached by a grim looking police training school commandant. "Your boys have gone a bit far this time." Usually he was a very pleasant man but he went on to explain that the housekeeper had complained that one entire section in bachelor quarters had been left in a shocking state, shaving foam and boot polish smeared all over bathrooms and toilets. It was our classes living accommodation so we had to deal with it.

I agree it was in a mess. After parade we read the riot act to them and gave them the chance for the guilty parties to own up, adding "if you're man enough."

When we returned the class rose, as was the custom. I told them that the guilty parties were to remain standing and the remainder could sit. Every single member of the class remained standing. Each one had admitted their part. It was the stag night of one of the course members.

Inwardly I felt that in a job, which demanded teamwork, this was a good example of future comradeship and support.

There wasn't much further we could go except to issue a stern warning as to their future conduct.

A part of the course that always created problems was the postings. A classic example of this was of a middle-aged family man, a Geordie who applied for Durham, Lower Newton and Frankland; all within reasonable distance of home and where did they post him? Isle of Wight.

He was nearly in tears when we saw him. "I like the job but I'm going to have to resign." We felt sorry for him because he appeared to have the makings of a good officer. After a few enquiries we found a lad who lived in the South who had been posted to Durham. With a little manipulation we arranged for a mutual exchange, both men jumped at the chance. This system proved popular so we extended it to anyone provided no pressure was exerted.

Just a little forethought could, I am sure have solved much hardship to the trainees and saved the department money.

We also made staff in training aware that tobacco had always been the major currency in prisons and any favours a prisoner required had to be purchased by handing over tobacco equivalent value to the price, which would normally be charged outside.

Lending to new inmates was one of the major areas where profit could be made easily. The person borrowing would think that the lender was being generous, but not at all, because the following week the collectors would be round, not asking but demanding repayment, not only of the loan but probably double.

The collectors were usually nasty, so called 'hard men' and if payment could not be met, so the interest would rise until the dept was impossible to repay. Roughly the going rate was £5.00 an ounce when I was in the service. This is the stage where a person would have to apply for protection, known inside as rule 43.

Rule 43 of the Prison Rules allowed a person to apply for constant protection, or for a governor to place a man on the rule if he considered that he was in danger, or putting others in danger, or likely to be a disruptive influence.

In America certain prisons made available tubs of loose tobacco from which prisoners could collect their weekly ration. Maybe this would have eliminated the profiteering because there would have been no need to borrow.

Tobacco had always dominated prison life and it was not until 1936 that all prisoners were permitted the so-called privilege. This was reserved for prisoners serving more than 4 years. With modern medical evidence, probably those who where serving under 4 years were more fortunate.

Cigarettes were known as roll ups and were probably only a quarter of the size of a normal cigarette. Matches were split into fours to make them last.

Old tobacco tins were covered and ornately decorated with photographs or fancy designs, sometimes incorporating a secret panel. Others were covered in used matches, varnished and laid out in the most intricate designs imaginable.

In the days of my earlier service, gas lights were situated on each landing and one day this little chap made a huge newspaper spill which he attempted to light the smallest dog end, the flame was enormous and how he didn't set himself ablaze I will never know.

Staff were warned not to soften and give prisoners cigarettes. I quoted myself as an example.

At one stage I was in a team taking a particularly violent character to Broadmoor. During the escort the man became very tense, it was during the time that I smoked. I thought that the best way to calm him was to give him a roll up. He appeared grateful. For some reason I logged this in my diary.

Several years later the man was certified as sane and eventually found his way back into prison. He singled me out and reminded me of the incident, threatening to inform on me to the Governor, I didn't give him the chance I put him straight before the Governor telling him of the incident and of my actions.

The Governor supported me and disciplined the man. To a weaker willed officer this could have led to his carrying out illegal acts for the prisoner and getting tangled up in a very nasty net indeed.

Again the highlighting of ones own experience gave a firm indicator to staff under training how they must operate to avoid pitfalls. "Do not enter a prisoners cell because a number of things could happen." This is how we addressed trainees during the initial officers training.

The cell and the landings were where many of the staff would work day in and day out. It would be the landing officer's job to unlock the cell doors and it was vitally important that they knew how to do it correctly, checking through what was known as the Judas Window first, to ensure where the prisoner(s) were positioned. The cell doors opened inwards so after unlocking, the main lock would be sprung thus reducing the danger of being grabbed and taken inside as a hostage and the door being slammed.

They were advised not to walk into the cell because of booby traps over the door, for example a full chamber pot over the door doesn't make an inviting shower especially before breakfast.

The other danger was of the door being shut on the officers arm and a cell door was extremely heavy and painful if it makes contact with you.

Trip wires were also used and if you entered through a door, I don't think that many of you would look on the floor before walking in.

All tricks of the trade and if you have experienced such obstructions then you don't forget again in a hurry.

This is why it was best to unlock, step back and let them sort themselves out because if the pot was to fall, then it would fall on them and they could only attack fresh air.

We provided practical demonstrations and if the students failed to carry out instructions they would get wet – very wet!

Despite the security aspect something, which had to be strictly borne in mind was that the cell was the prisoners home, it was the place where the person would sleep, eat, study, read, think, cry and sometimes pray, so landing staff would have to also be sensitive to this.

It jokingly shows cartoon prisoners vanishing and the bars being sawn through. It's not a joke and daily the locks, bolts and bars were checked. So as can be seen cells play a large part in the every day bread and butter work of a prison officer.

Handcuffing

"Never cuff the prisoner first because if you do you will regret it." This was our opening sentence to trainee officers. Again there is a right and wrong way. The reason for this opening piece of advice was simply that you will have provided a nasty weapon. The correct way would be to secure the cuff to the escorting officer's wrist and hope that he held nothing against you.

It was also good policy to fit the cuffs standing behind the prisoner and stand sideways on to reduce any potential target area.

Most of the instructors had worked at the sharp end and probably some had experienced attacks by the reluctant prisoner. I knew, I had.

If it was a longish escort then the officer had to carry what was known as a closeting chain*, basically an extension to a wrist cuff designed to enable a man to attend the toilet in private but still maintaining security.

If a person had very slim wrists then inserts were used to ensure they fitted securely, although despite this I have known one person slip - even

* See illustration twelve "closeting chain"

with the inserts - his wrist was so small. Fortunately he did this just to show that it was possible.

The two most important exercises as far as prison staff were concerned involved cell searches and the removal of a violent prisoner barricaded in a cell. Both of these events were treated very seriously because in reality someone could end up either badly hurt or worse, if either of these situations were handled incorrectly.

For the purpose of this we used to transport the class members by coach to Preston prison and make use of a suite of unoccupied cells, where they could scream and shout to their hearts content and not be heard.

For the cell search we would secrete a number of items ranging from a knife to a hacksaw in the various nooks and crannies within the cell. Most of the items were discovered following a thorough search as taught, but one always remained untouched in its original hiding place.

The trainees would search very carefully but would ignore the chamber pot, which was well past its sell-by-date. To make it more realistic the pot contained some evil looking liquid with two corks in, both painted brown – suffice to say it looked very real.

After being asked if they had searched the entire cell and us being reassured they had. One of us would plunge a hand into the chamber pot amidst gasps and groans from the group and withdraw a bundle of tightly bound cloth, opened it to reveal a 38 revolver and a clip of bullets.

This wasn't intended to belittle anyone, but to emphasise the point that the place missed could be the one where the vital item is hidden.

For the second exercise we would select very strong people, give them enough time to barricade themselves in the cell, then select teams of three to remove them applying the techniques they had been trained to use.

If they applied the holds correctly they could use them against anyone, no matter how violent they were and restrain them with a minimum amount of force.

When they had successfully completed an evacuation it was an enormous boost to their self -confidence.

The only time I have ever seen this system fail was when an officer, who was a national tug-of-war champion played the part of the prisoner and despite any efforts, no-one could keep him in the holds. He would allow staff to apply the locks and then break both wrist locks and a head hold by sending staff scattering like nine pins, disillusioning to say the least, but probably his wrists held more strength than I had in my entire body. He was a gentle giant.

As the students gained more knowledge they were given a written test before being allowed home on weekend breaks. They became very proficient at these and competition became quite fierce between other classes. Most of the questions were based on the week's lessons with the odd few thrown in as red herrings.

Courses tended to fly by and before we knew it, it was the end of course dinner, over the nine weeks the individual classes used to save up and take their instructors out for the evening.

At one of these evenings after eating the meal, we prepared to go into the bar. A lady who was busily clearing the tables asked us who we were. She was told and said that her son was a prison officer at Dartmoor prison and if we stayed behind we could have a good laugh, because it was the managers birthday and a strip-o-gram had been organised.

The boys then decided to stay behind. In walks this object – supposed to be a policeman – some policeman, with brown shoes and a silver paper badge on his cap. They in turn decided to have their own share of fun by nominating me as the manager, despite my protests and anger. However, when he called for assistance in walked an extremely attractive police lady, my group told them that I was not in fact the manager and where the true manager was.

My group thought this was hilarious but I didn't and half angry and half embarrassed I threatened to even the scores on the parade square despite the following days hangover. "Us fitting you up Mr P, after all the things you have pulled on us for nine weeks." "All we are doing is getting a little of our own back." After thinking about this I came to the conclusion that maybe they were right and I would forget it, but didn't let on to them.

The following morning I think that the king-sized hangovers some were nursing was sufficient punishment, so after a strict inspection and once round the square I let them go.

Whilst on the course we met up with some very high ranking members of the Sri Lanka Police, who were on an advanced driving course, we got to know them very well. One commented one day, "Why we are on an advanced drivers course I don't know! We haven't even got any bloody decent roads." Food for thought isn't it.

However, after two excellent courses working with some very nice people we were on our way back.

A NEW CHALLENGE

Foston Hall

Upon my return from the training school I was advised that I was to take over a satellite of Sudbury prison, namely Foston Hall.

If I can take you back many years, in its history Foston Hall started life in Jacobean times and the current building is the fourth one to stand on the site.

In the past, several aristocratic families had used it as a stately home but more recently it had been used as a railway orphanage, a detention centre, and immigration holding camp. Now it was to take on a role as an educational centre catering for mainly long-term prisoners, including some serving life.

It was to provide teaching, ranging from the very basic educational needs through to degree standard. The system was to prove popular with all levels and the basic student was equally as proud of his achievements as the man attaining a BSc or a Masters degree.

Computer skills were highly popular and consequently business study courses were always well attended. Some attended University; others worked at outside jobs mostly on farms, but also some in local industry.

It was quite strange to see the prison slowly empty each morning and fill up again at night.

Some courses had to be carefully monitored, because what better opportunity for carrying illegal items into or out of the prison than by using people, who were on an outside, unsupervised job or attending colleges.

Strangely enough this freedom was not too often abused, at least to our knowledge because many had too much to lose, especially lifers.

Those who did chance their luck tried various methods to traffic, smuggle goods in, but the regular searches that took place acted as a constant deterrent with inmates not knowing where, or who would be the next one to be searched.

Others, before entering the prison would hide things in the bushes and ditches outside to be collected by a runner later, or to be collected by an outside worker on the following morning. The only danger to this was, of staff discovering the items before prisoners could collect, because we regularly deployed officers to patrol the outer perimeter fences.

If the more affluent had items brought in and secreted they would pay someone else to do their dirty work for them. Very low rates were offered and if they were caught, they would be expected to take the consequences.

Sometimes we found illegal items, but in my opinion we only just scratched the surface. The only deterrent we could provide was by constantly searching, which at least kept them on their toes and uncertain of our next move, so less likely to take a chance.

No matter how much we carried out this policy there would always remain those who would try to beat the system.

Main items would of course be drugs, tobacco and alcohol, but also actual cash. One man was using stolen credit cards to draw money, another was even suspected of organising a robbery in a village branch of a bank. This was never proved, but I'm sure that there was some substance in these suspicions. Some of course, used to meet their wives and sweethearts for other purposes?

A constant worry for anyone in charge of Foston, would be the fire risk and even more so in a building with so much dry timber it would have gone up like a tinder box, it was for this reason that regular fire drills were held. Everyone, without exception was expected to evacuate immediately, assemble at the designated spot where they would be checked off and the whole operation timed. Of course the usual idiots were not in the slightest interested and failed to attend until being chased by staff.

I used to tell them, they had been burned to death but re-incarnated, and they would then be allowed to return to normal activities, grinning as they walked away. We would let them just settle down and repeat the entire drill over again. They soon got the message.

Whilst talking of wood, some of the carvings were magnificent. One item I can readily call to mind was a fine example by a well-known wood carver named 'Gringling Gibbons,' which was an oak fireplace extending from floor to ceiling in the main office. It was intricately carved containing every type of wild life and produce.

Apparently always at the bottom of this mans carvings was a pea pod. This indicated if at the time of purchase the debt had been paid. If the pod was open then the carver had to be paid, but if it was closed the debt had been settled.

As would be expected in a building as historical as this, it had its share of ghost stories. The main one was of the Grey Lady, who was said to return to search for her son who had failed to return from the Civil War.

I didn't see her but one of my night officers used to say that he saw and talked to her regularly. He has now joined her, so we'll never know the truth! All I was aware of was a change in temperature when entering a certain part of the building.

Many of the buildings windows were of plate glass and again extended from floor to ceiling in many places.

One day I was watching a football match, the game looked good and I had decided to go outside to get a better view, however some matter delayed me and in this period of time there was an enormous crash. A large pane of broken glass speared its way down and shattered on the very area of the terrace I would have been standing in if I had ventured out. A prisoner resident in the room directly above us felt that he could take no more and hurled a chair across the room, hitting and smashing the window and as it broke the jagged pieces crashed outside onto the ground below.

Had I been standing there then it was a very unlikely for me to be writing this book today, because I would have probably been decapitated. Certainly, once again someone was on my side that day and many more.

Prisoners seemed to wish to raise funds for charity by taking part in marathon events. Two I recall were a sponsored bridge contest, the funds of which were given to the Royal School of the Deaf, a marathon run donation was made to other organisations including Children in Need and the Children's Hospital in Derby.

On several occasions I was given the privilege of handing over the cheque including one to the local radio station.

These were quite large donations, but the largest organised event to take place at Foston was to deliver a lorry load of goods and supplies to Bosnia. Items were collected from all over Britain from hospitals, industry, sporting clubs and a variety of departmental stores. My contribution towards this was only management, but the keenness shown by those involved reached virtual fever pitch.

A small group, including a haulier who was serving a sentence, overseen by a group of dedicated officers did much of the wheeling and dealing. My phone was from where most of the deals were organised and each time I answered the call they seemed to be relating to the appeal.

Storage space was at a premium and every vacant space was crammed with items ranging from toilet rolls to beds.

The vehicle was a large Volvo lorry and was to be driven by an officer who was an experienced driver. The media gave the project plenty of publicity, both locally and nationally and well-known businesses were keen to sponsor.

To say the trip went without a hitch would not be true because the driver experienced several problems, especially from border guards each wishing for their cut, before allowing the vehicle to proceed to the next stage. However, the trip was successfully completed and the driver arrived safely back.

This trip, although far removed from the day to day routine of prison life, proves that there is good in many people despite past backgrounds.

Before I was allowed to deal with daily applications, we used to have a Governor visit around lunchtime to take prisoners requests. One day, whilst the Governor and a member of staff had all been members of the same choir, we were talking about the past when the Governor said, "Do you both remember all things bright and beautiful, the descant part?" We both said we did. "OK," the Governor replied. "On the count of three." At which time they all burst into song. I had to quickly leave the room and the inmates in the queue also looked bewildered. I think that they hoped that they weren't going to be asked the same questions.

Another part of the Governor's routine was to test the various diets before prisoners ate them, if it was either poisoned or bad the Governor would be the first to go. Mostly it was to counteract frivolous complaints.

The meals generally were very good and adequate and the cooks excelled themselves, especially on Bank Holidays and during the weekends.

Prison caterers underwent a stiff training course over several months and then had to pass City and Guilds qualifications, but above everything else they were prison officers as were all specialists in the service.

There were many diets in prison, ranging from Medical to Religious, but one that somehow seemed to be more of a problem than most was the Fast of Ramadan.

Participants were permitted their two meals to be taken between Sunset and Sunrise, which were cooked by themselves under officer supervision. The movement in the small hours obviously disturbed sleeping inmates, which didn't go down too well with the other occupants and often caused friction.

At the end of the period a big feast took place with the Imam bringing in special food. An invitation was extended to us. The meal was something like our Christmas dinner, but with an Asian style of food. I was sceptical at first, but readily accepted any subsequent invites because the food was really tasty.

Situated within the prison was an ornamental fishpond that was well stocked with fish of various sorts. It was looked after by a man, who besides helping to supply the fish, was in his own right an expert on them.

Unfortunately someone in our midst did not share the same point of view and for some futile reason one night deposited a large amount of detergent liquid in the pond, killing the entire contents of the pond.

The person strongly suspected absconded, which was as well for him, because had he have remained I think survival would have been very difficult against the remainder of inmates, judging their mood at the time.

Amongst the many sports activities, running seemed to be one of the most popular and some officers had formed a small club. Carefully selected inmates were taken out during lunchtimes around the country lanes and back roads. Members of this club prided themselves at being chosen and trusted. To my knowledge this trust was never flaunted.

To some people this sort of activity should not be allowed, but to this I would argue that without being given degrees of trust how can judgement be made as to consideration for future release, which sooner or later will happen anyway. Running inside the prison was also popular and some would run around the sports field for hours.

One day a slightly built elderly man who had just arrived joined them. The big boys started to show off their skills and fitness. Many laps later he was still with them running at steady pace. As the circuits went by, the so called, 'big boys' started to flag, this little man was still going, lapping each one of the others in turn until all had dropped out. He still kept going for many laps more. They looked on in disbelief, as they did not know that the man they started showing off too, was in fact an Olympic representative in years gone by. Another case for not judging the book by its cover.

I often see him now; he devotes much of his time to transporting the sick to and from hospital.

He had his sentence quashed by the Court of Appeal and if anyone deserved it, he did. However we missed his tea.

In our service staff came from all walks of life and Foston was no exception. There were ex-servicemen, footplate men, a dental mechanic, miners and a whole host of others. This to a large extent helped, especially in the individual case officer situations, when certain prisoners would often only relate to people who in their view had something in common with them.

The ex-dental mechanic, a popular member of staff attracted much attention because as well as being a senior member of staff he was also a member of the Magic Circle, the International Brotherhood of Magicians. He was a very able conjurer and a born comedian. To accompany him in his act he had a toy racoon and what he couldn't make this animal do, was not worth doing.

I recall on one occasion, one of the PEI's was making some derogatory remark where upon he burst into a flood of tears. The PEI feeling he had gone too far went over to console him, only to find that the tears were something he could produce at will and our conjuror burst into laughter. He was putting on an act.

Whilst we had taken what in our view were sufficient steps to curtail contraband smuggling, another type of fraud was beginning to take place.

A minority of computer students had been misusing the system. In prison the continuation of business was illegal, it wasn't illegal to hand over the running of a business, or to wind one down, but only to run one.

This particular prisoner was secretly using all of our facilities to run his business, including our private address for many clients to write to him, the latter being unaware that the contact point was a prison. He even gave them our telephone and fax numbers. Quietly but confidently he was building up a nice little business at the expense of the education department. We quickly stamped this out and warned the others against operating this practice, the computer experts, took steps to monitor the systems.

The case officer system was running well also being extended to town and leisure visits. Staff were very interested in participating and in general the prisoners rarely took any advantage. Of course, the occasional one did by slipping his escort. For the majority however they respected this liberty.

The lifers especially had much to lose, it could give them extra years on top of their proposed license date, so it wasn't worth it, secondly they would not wish to let their respective case officers down.

Those who did abscond usually were on the last part of a sentence and we found it very hard to understand why! We felt that insecurity was probably the reason and not being able to face the outside world after being inside for so long.

The next step from Open Prison would be a period in the hostel scheme. For 6-12 months, during which time they would be allowed more freedom than an Open Prison offered. Upon arrival they would probably be detailed to cooking and cleaning duties within the hostel and with the help of the Warden go in search of employment. They would then earn a normal working wage and at the end of each week were required to surrender their wages to the Warden who would allocate spending money, savings and deduct the cost of their keep.

Most weekends they would go home and were allowed out in the evenings, but had to return before a certain time.

During this crucial period they were carefully monitored and were still subject to prison rules, despite the fact that they were living in the hostel, which was always outside of the prison. This stage was vital, particularly to lifers because breaching their conditions could mean being returned to prison.

At Foston Hall we had a few trade training courses, one of which was the overhaul and servicing of lawnmowers. We were able to have our mowers serviced upon payment of a fee, so I took advantage and had my hover mower serviced. When it was returned, I couldn't wait to try it out, however it was nearly the last time I got to use it. As I pulled the operating lever there was a flash followed by a bang, I quickly let it go and switched off. I returned the machine and after the wiring was checked; it had been fitted incorrectly. Deliberate or accident, I'm unsure, but I quickly got rid and ever since have stuck to a push mower, it's safer - and keeps you fitter!

Our routine accommodation inspections were strict, more than in the larger parent prisons and the relatively smaller numbers usually produced much higher standards. The others usually quickly sorted out any occupant who wasn't pulling their weight.

Often the cook's room was the worst; probably the reason was due to the fact that they were very early risers in order to prepare breakfast. Usually they would put things right during their break, if not they would face the wrath of either myself or one of my colleagues. Of course, if you upset the cooks you would have to exercise extreme caution when testing the meal. Just in case!

In a small community such as ours, staff participation was encouraged and quite often an officer would compete against the inmates, at pool, table tennis or darts, frequently beating their opponents. This often helped to build up good relationships and in turn produced a better response during interviews; it was a question of trust by both parties.

Whilst talking of indoor games, care had to be taken to ensure that gambling was prevented, especially to any large degree.

One morning I had a young man apply for a transfer to another prison, I could see that he was extremely nervous and very agitated. I enquired as to his reason for wanting to move. He explained, that during the weekend he had become involved in a 'double or quits' racket and being gullible he went along trying to wipe out his debt. However by continuing in this vein he finishing up owing hundreds of Mars Bars.

It transpired that a pool hustler, who knew that he was certain to win, kept doubling the stake and had him hooked.

We quickly moved the hustler out of the prison and had no further trouble. It just shows what can happen when things are allowed to get out of hand. Seemingly innocent to start with, but turning nasty as time progresses.

Ship outs took place quickly, for a variety of reasons. Those who were unable to cope, being disruptive, vandals, bullies or attempted strong-arm tactics, also those who we felt were liable to abscond.

An old lifer, who was an expert at reading upside down, knew of his release even before I informed him officially. His claim to fame was that he held the most GCE's, O and A Levels in the country. For this he secured a place in the Guinness Books of Records. I'm not sure exactly how many but it was close to fifty.

It all arose from when he was first sentenced; the Prisons Education Officer told him that he was too old to be considered for study. Determined to show them just how wrong they were, he studied every conceivable subject imaginable and the rest is history.

Some of the artistic talents prisoners possessed was unbelievable, had they been put to better use there could have been many successes rather than failures through criminal activity.

Foston was a way of life rather than a job. Certainly it presented a big challenge, not only to us, but also to the inmates. Bearing in mind that this step was to them probably the most important one taken for many years, with all eyes upon them and their every move. This was the time, which could make or break them.

Just as I was about to retire, they published in their own magazine words to the effect that I had strayed from the normal run of the mill prison regime. Creating a relaxed uncomplicated atmosphere, in which inmates and officers alike could interact with the role of education.

It was teamwork that produced this, not just me. Most of the work had been done before I arrived, I just continued it. To begin with the routine wasn't easy to operate, it produced many problems, comments including a familiar phrase, 'I told you that wouldn't work' was one used by the cynics, but strangely enough usually it did work. Despite their comments the routine gained ground rapidly and the system began to operate like a well-oiled machine.

It wasn't long after this that I was returned to Sudbury, retaining a supervisory role for Foston Hall. I enjoyed working at all my postings but Foston Hall held something special for me, maybe it was the staff, the building or the challenge, who knows?

The establishment is now a female prison and I wish the current Governor every success. I hope that she enjoys her stay as much as I did and from reading local news comments she has already taken some positive steps forward. I am pleased to see that it is not going to rack and ruin, as was first thought, but being put to good use for an important purpose.

Private Sector

Just before I retired a colleague of mine put forward what appeared a very attractive proposition. I say appeared, because it didn't turn out as proposed.

The Government were privatising the running of courts and escorts. The company taking on this contract were keen to recruit experienced staff to assist in setting the system up. Would I be interested in helping to organise the training of new staff? It sounded interesting to me and another challenge, not to mention the salary, so I accepted.

I was soon to discover that the whole operation was police orientated and the system geared to work via police methods. Not that I object to this, but people in custody were so used to prison procedures that I visualised there being some problems, to say the least.

We tried to incorporate into the training programme as much as possible of the prison services court working practices, but as to how this would turn out we would have to wait and see.

As many people will know, the first day was absolute chaos, with us being the butt of many cartoons appearing in the following few days newspapers.

I feel that much could have been done to make it an easier passage, but of course, privatisation was a dirty word in certain areas, especially the police and prison services, who could blame them! It may cut costs and make private care in custody more important than reaching targets.

Teething troubles did occur, with escapes, late arrivals at court and disruption by prisoners being amongst the main problems. Others were relating to conditions, food and property. If a chance arises then prisoners will always try to take advantage of the situation and seeing these men and woman attired in black blazers and grey trousers, or some girls preferred skirts, it didn't matter which! Who better to try their luck to con, they weren't screws, so we'll have a go. This was their thinking, although I'm convinced some were put up to it.

216

Complaints, such as the food is cold, we want to buy food from McDonalds from our own money, the cells are crowded, there's no air, we want the door left open, my jackets damaged, I want compensation, my cash is short, caused staff many headaches. The old prison officers amongst the team told them where to get off, in fact they didn't try it on with them, just the ones who were not used to the system.

Most of the judiciary were sympathetic towards all the possible pit falls this would produce in its early stages, but some weren't, especially older and very senior judges. Excuses were not in their book and I genuinely felt sorry for some of the senior staff, who had to face the wrath of their lordships.

It seems that the system has settled down and the companies are coping adequately. However, my opinion doesn't change in that, you would not expect a tailor to carry the work of a steeple jack and likewise, I would not expect the of a security company to equip them to immediately carry out the duties of police or prison officers, who have had years of experience. Conversely for prisoners who for so many years had responded to the uniformed prison staff to accept the change to being controlled by staff wearing blazer and flannels, without meeting some degree of resistance or at least, trying their hand at it.

I HEARD IT ON THE RADIO,
SO IT MUST BE TRUE

As one approaches the end of their chosen career, there is always a tendency to have certain mis-givings and doubts about the past and whether you have coped.

Questions arise as to the choice made, whether or not it was the right one to make and reflections as to how you handled certain situations over the years.

Looking at this in all honesty, I would say that the choice of job for me was probably right in the long term, but initially, I only entered into it because I was trying to improve a botched up past and to make amends. I had until been restless, constantly moving and changing jobs and realised that the time had arrived for me to settle down and make ago of things.

I have tried to give my all to the job, perhaps sometimes too much, for which, I sacrificed family life. This I would definitely never do again, especially the upheaval of moving.

I certainly would have tackled some areas differently, but think that by and large I have managed effectively. Any manager knows that they are only as good as the staff will allow and that the people on the ground floor are the most important. Thankfully, I had a great team and was indebted to them. the saying is that every barrel has its bad apple. I found to be untrue, or lucky because I didn't have one.

There wasn't anything spectacular about my retirement day, it was the same as any other, none of my charges knew I was going, only staff. The day was uneventful as routine days go and the final evening duty passed very quickly. I accepted the locking up figures and handed over to the night shift.

I took my team for a quiet drink and then drove home after having said my farewells. I didn't feel retired, it was just imagination and tomorrow I would be back to the same old routine again. Getting up early and coming home late.

I parked the car and sat drinking a cup of tea which was always ready, rain or shine – bless her. We were quiet and listening to late night local radio and as we sat there the broadcaster gave out a message from my staff wishing us good luck for the future. It was only then that it hit home, I would not be getting up early or returning to duty ever again. I had truly retired.